A Platonic Philosophy of Religion

A Platonic Philosophy of Religion

A Process Perspective

Daniel A. Dombrowski

State University of New York Press

Published by

State University of New York Press, Albany

Printed in the United States of America

For information, address State University of New York Press,
90 State Street, Suite 700, Albany, NY 12207

Production by Michael Haggett
Marketing by Michael Campochiaro

Library of Congress Cataloging-in-Publication Data

Dombrowski, Daniel A.
    A platonic philosophy of religion : a process perspective / by
Daniel A. Dombrowski.
        p. cm.
    Includes bibliographical references and index.
    ISBN 0-7914-6283-8 (hardcover : alk. paper)
    ISBN 0-7914-6284-6 (pbk. : alk. paper)
    1. Religion—Philosophy. 2. Plato. I. Title.

BL51.D555   2005
210—dc22   2004016639

10 9 8 7 6 5 4 3 2 1

Contents

Acknowledgments

Chapter 1 relies largely on a previously published article titled "Taking the World Soul Seriously," *The Modern Schoolman* 69 (1991): 33–57; and chapter 2 relies largely on an article titled "Being *Is* Power," *American Journal of Theology & Philosophy* 16 (1995): 299–314.

Introduction

The Inevitable Question

Alfred North Whitehead is famous for his observation that "the safest general characterization of the European philosophical tradition is that it consists of a series of footnotes to Plato."[1] This safety is due, in part, to the fact that Plato is an "inexhaustible mine" of ideas such that, when one seam runs out, a richer one is struck, as if by magic. The chief error not only in Plato scholarship, Whitehead thinks, but also in philosophy in general, is overstatement. This most often occurs when one facet of the subject matter in question is mistaken for the whole. The goal of the present book is to provide a counterbalance to previous treatments of Plato's thoughts on God that overstate the case for his ontolatry; that is, for his worship of being as opposed to becoming.

I assume that Whitehead's intent in the above quotation is not to denigrate philosophers subsequent to Plato by calling them mere "footnotes" but rather to emphasize the wealth of ideas in Plato, an abundance that is especially evident concerning religious questions.[2] Of course many people, including many philosophers, will not be impressed with the claim that Plato provides a cornucopia of ideas. They will ask what Nicholas Smith calls "the inevitable question": what more could be said about Plato that has not been said after two and a half millennia of commentary?[3]

Smith is correct in rejecting one easy, relativist answer to this question, that each generation of scholars must reinterpret the Greeks in terms that are acceptable for their own time. The problems Smith notices in this response are that (1) scholars are discovering, or think that they are discovering, some truths about Plato's dialogues that previous scholars had not noticed; and as a result (2) progress can occur in the understanding of Plato's writings. Scholarly pursuits sometimes *do* need periodic updating, as in the case noted by Smith where the works of perfectly competent nineteenth-century translators need to be updated because they do not work for us in the twenty-first century. But the updating should always be guided by the desire

1

for intellectual progress. Something like this is at work in the present book in that the twentieth-century intellectual movement called "process philosophy of religion" or "process theism" enables us to see new things in Plato's dialogues themselves or at least to see them more clearly than they were seen before. But this is a far cry from reinventing Plato or creating a new, ersatz Plato for the purposes of contemporary philosophy of religion.

The allusion on Smith's part to the story of the three blindfolded investigators who examine an elephant is also helpful: one feels the trunk and thinks it is a snake, one feels the elephant's side and thinks it is a wall, and a third feels the tail and thinks it is a rope. The hermeneutical difficulty here is primarily one of scope. The partial remedy for this difficulty would seem to be for the three investigators to exchange places with each other such that a more accurate description of the elephant could be obtained. Once again, something like this procedure is aimed at in the present book. That is, in addition to the valuable perspectives provided by many Plato scholars who are analytic philosophers, and by continental philosophers such as Heidegger, Gadamer, and others, there are the perspectives of several process philosophers or neoclassical metaphysicians that should be taken seriously. The present book is an attempt to explicate and defend this family of Plato interpreters, among whom are Whitehead himself, Charles Hartshorne, Henri Bergson, John Cobb, David Ray Griffin, Robert Neville, and Leonard Eslick.

Of course the corrective standpoint on Plato's conception of God provided by process thinkers is not necessarily the final word on the topic. To follow through on Smith's elephant metaphor, it is better to examine the trunk, the tail, and the side of the elephant rather than only one or two of these, but there are still the ears, the toes, and so on, of the elephant that could help us to provide a richer account. But this admission of fallibilism does not prevent us from noticing the influence of the power structure of academe on how Plato scholarship is done. As Smith puts the point:

> [M]any potentially edifying controversies are suffocated before they can become matters of general discussion. Consensus is all too often reached, instead, through neglect. ... [W]e tend to conceive of the issues in too narrow a way; because we tend to focus on and be focused by the points of view promoted by those with the highest status in the profession; because we get caught up in interpretive fads; and because we tend to ask only questions that reflect our own narrow preoccupations or interests.[4]

My thesis is that the process perspective(s) on Plato's view of God have largely been neglected and that this neglect impoverishes both our view of

Plato *and* our view of what could be said in contemporary philosophy of religion on a Platonic basis.

At least some of the disputes in scholarship regarding Plato's view of God can be resolved by appeal to the primary texts, but even if all parties cite the texts accurately there is the possibility (even the likelihood) of continued disagreement due to the conflicting principles of interpretation assumed by the scholars in question. In the present book I will exhibit both traditional textual exposition and argumentation from contemporary (process) philosophy of religion. No doubt some scholars will disagree with the latter, but at least my cards will be on the table for all to see, an openness that is meant to facilitate Popperian criticism in an open society of Plato scholars and of scholars in philosophy of religion.

It is somewhat disconcerting, however, to notice how little philosophers read across the conceptual borders of their own method or style of doing philosophy. Hartshorne once complained about this phenomenon in the following terms: "I feel somewhat bitter often because philosophers do so little honest facing of each others' criticisms. ... Is philosophy a rational discipline, or is it self-defense of one's own castle of ideas?"[5]

One of the difficulties in getting a hearing for a process or neoclassical theistic interpretation of Plato is resistance in some circles to metaphysics itself or to theism. Such resistance is especially odd for a Plato scholar, given the prominence of God and of metaphysical issues in Plato's writings. In any event, Giovanni Reale seems to exaggerate a bit when he calls the Tubingen school of Plato scholars, of which he is a member, the "most metaphysically oriented" approach to Plato in modern times in that the process approach to Plato is equally concerned with metaphysical issues and with Plato's view of God.[6]

Later in the book I will cite a quotation from Josiah Royce to the effect that we contemporary thinkers are not as original as we often think. That is, thought about God is historical thinking in the sense that we never start thinking of God *de novo* but are always reacting to or modifying the concept(s) of 'God' that have been passed down from generation to generation. No thinker has been more influential in the development of the Western concept(s) of God than Plato, hence there is something bold in the process claim that most, but not all, interpreters of Plato's theism over the centuries have either not noticed or have underemphasized, the *dynamism* of his theism.

The classicist Walter Burkert agrees that there is no theology that has not stood in Plato's shadow, whether in the Judeo-Christian West or in the Islamic East. In fact, the aura of Christianity that attaches to Plato has been something of an embarrassment for some classicists. This "aura" surrounds the supposedly firm Platonic beliefs that (1) "this" material reality is made somewhat unreal in the face of an incorporeal, unchangeable "other" world that is to be regarded as primary and in some sense divine; and (2) the ego is "concentrated in an immortal soul which is alien to the body and captive in it."[7] These beliefs were anticipated by those in the Orphic cults, by Parmenides, and by developments in mathematics made by the Pythagoreans, but Plato, it is alleged, perfected them. On this view, Platonism just *is* the bifurcation of reality into the changeable and the unchangeable, with the latter (which contains some confused mixture of the divine Nous and the forms) superior to the former.

Although Burkert is not explicit in his criticisms of this view of Plato, he does implicitly point the way toward a critical assessment of it. For example, he notes that the concept of 'divine omnipotence' does not enter into Plato's philosophy of being, which suggests that God *becomes* in relation to the creatures, as we will see. Burkert also endorses the idea, crucial in the present book, that in Plato's later dialogues there is self-criticism of some of Plato's earlier concepts such that, to use Burkert's somewhat confusing language, Plato is seen as "introducing movement into being."[8] The avenue for such introduction is the attribution of cosmic status to soul, as we will see in chapter 1 concerning God as the World Soul. Lesser gods or *daimones*, on Burkert's reading, are "introduced in a playfully ironic note."[9]

Much in Burkert's view is compatible with the process interpretation of Plato, say as found in Whitehead's frequent allusions to the *Timaeus* and to A. E. Taylor's commentary on that work. On this interpretation, God is more like the Platonic (or biblical) Demiurge than like an omnipotent Caesar. (The relationship between Plato's Demiurge and the World Soul will be treated in detail later.) It must be admitted that Whitehead saw Plato as a "muddle-headed" thinker, but in Whitehead's scheme of things this is a compliment in that, by way of contrast, "clear-headed" thinkers often overlook the complexity and subtlety of the truth.[10] One of these subtleties, according to Whitehead, concerns the identification of being with *dynamis* or dynamic power in the *Sophist*. Another is the distinction in the *Philebus* between the limit (*peras*) and the unlimit (*apeiron*), which roughly corresponds to the cosmological factors of the forms and the receptacle, respectively, in the *Timaeus*: the mixed (*micton*) is a compound of these two principles as we find it in the world of becoming. It is difficult to see Plato as a systematic philosopher not merely because he wrote in dialogue form but also because he tried to catch every aspect of the universe in his theories.[11]

Perhaps partially because of Plato's reticulation, he has been variously interpreted. Robert O'Connell is correct in noting the healthiness in a certain skepticism regarding the standard Judeo-Christian interpretation of Plato over the centuries, but he is also correct in noting that recently the pendulum has swung to the opposite extreme. We might end up with a sort of paralysis regarding what Plato says about God, the gods, or divine things like the forms, due to a fear of the claim that Plato was at base a theist.[12] Clearly the Greek word *theos* provides a problem for interpreters. For example, there is the well-known view of German philologists that '*theos*' primarily had a predicative force, as when those occurrences that especially awed the Greeks were seen in religious terms, as in "loving is *theos*." The extent to which, and the ways in which, this claim is similar to the Johannine view that "God is love" is open to scholarly discussion. On the process view that I am defending in the present book, the gap between these two statements can to a great extent be minimized. That is, a process interpretation of Plato can help to combat a scholarly inertia that has arisen with respect to the relationship between Plato's theism and that in Western religions.

Consider the highly influential view of G. M. A. Grube, who contrasts the dynamism of the Greek *theos* with the more reified, yet supposedly personal, deity of many contemporary theists.[13] In the course of the present book we will see that this contrast can be called into question both because of the surprisingly personal elements that can be detected in Plato's theism and because of the dynamism that can be found in certain (neoclassical) versions of contemporary theism.

ASYMMETRICALITY IN THE DIALOGUES

Because of his famous aforementioned remark that all of Western philosophy can best be seen as a series of footnotes to Plato, and because of his equally famous defense of eternal objects, Whitehead is often thought of as a Platonist. Yet despite Hartshorne's use of Plato's thoughts on the World Soul in the *Timaeus* and elsewhere, he is hardly ever compared to Plato because he is some sort of critic of eternal objects. But Hartshorne is every bit as much the Platonist as Whitehead, as we will see.

The word *Platonist* is assuredly vague, however. Hartshorne himself is very much aware that the dialogue format suggests little intention of formal unity and that implicit in the character of Socrates is a denial of rigid system. Although a completely satisfactory resolution to the problem of whether there really is one Platonic philosophy will continue to elude scholars, there is nonetheless sufficient unity of an informal type that one can talk of a philosopher as a Platonist. At least three different approaches to Plato can be imagined: (1) The dialogues can be considered stages in the intellectual development of Plato, whereby if one looks at Plato's later dialogues one finds the most significant account of his position.[14] (2) The dialogues can be viewed as complex aspects of a unified system, such that the content of all the dialogues must be unified in any systematic interpretation of Plato.[15] And (3), the dialogues may merely express a set of loosely related and perhaps conflicting themes such that no relational whole may be found.

Hartshorne favors the first of these three views. The principles in the early dialogues are retained in the later, but they are used within a more profound system of concepts, just as Plato's thoughts can be used by neoclassical metaphysicians like Hartshorne without Plato being affected by their speculation. (It should also be noted that Hartshorne's thoughts on the asymmetricality of Plato's dialogues are perhaps the best clues we have as to how Hartshorne would have us regard his own philosophic career, particularly the flurry of works he published after he turned seventy.[16]) Hartshorne traces Plato's development through three periods: the early dialogues up to and including the *Republic*; the Eleatic dialogues, where the "system" of the *Republic* is criticized; and the later dialogues, particularly the *Timaeus* and *Laws*. The traditional objections to Plato's philosophy do not apply with the same force by the time we reach the later dialogues; and it is no accident for Hartshorne that it is in these dialogues that God becomes a central concern for Plato. Although it is too simplistic to say that there is an inverse relationship between the emphasis placed on the theory of forms and that placed on God, it does seem fair to say that there is a shift in meaning in Plato's thought when teleological explanation according to forms is modified by teleological explanation in terms of God.

Obviously Hartshorne is not the sort of historian of philosophy (nor is Whitehead) who offers detailed textual arguments in favor of his appropriation of an author.[17] Rather, he seems to exemplify the dictum that the purpose of doing history of philosophy is to serve present philosophizing and life, not the other way around. And his thoughts on Plato should be evaluated according to this standard.

One fruitful result of Hartshorne's thesis regarding the asymmetricality of the dialogues is that it offers a mode of resolving the seemingly interminable debates regarding the question of system in Plato. The final dialogues retain in *some* fashion all of the categories of the earlier dialogues, such that with a bit of qualification the second view of Plato mentioned above can be seen as an adjunct or internal corrective agent to the first. So also, alternate principles of explanation lead to alternate conceptions of soul and God; hence conflicts appear, which easily lead many scholars to posit a particular dialogue as early or late. But these conflicts are often found in the final dialogues themselves, making it possible to claim that the third position mentioned above is virtually contained in the first. These tensions in Plato's thought should not cause astonishment (or deconstructionist anarchy) but rather should give us the confidence in the philosophical adequacy of Plato's thought in that he elaborated all (or most of) the necessary themes to do philosophy well *now*.[18]

My assumption throughout the book is that it is possible to have philosophical progress. But such progress is perfectly consistent with some sort of regress. That is, the mature Plato discovered much in philosophy of religion that was lost in the Middle Ages and in the Reformation, such that today we can be animated by the exciting prospect of rereading Plato so as to discover the religious richness of his later dialogues. In effect, there are two Platos in philosophy of religion, according to Hartshorne:

> [There is the] Plato that most philosophers think that they know, and then there's the Plato that they [do not] know. Plato said, "In God there is being and becoming," so he did not disagree with the Jews about that. The fact that that is overlooked by so many Christians and Islamic people, seems to me to be a very important regression in the history of philosophy. Plato didn't say that God is unchanging. Not at all. He said that there is change in God.[19]

Throughout the book I will attempt to dot each *i* and cross each *t* in Hartshorne's stance. My hope is that I will bridge the gap between (1) process thinkers such as Whitehead and Hartshorne, who are great admirers of Plato's view of God but do not offer detailed textual analysis of the relevant passages in Plato and (2) classicists and historians of philosophy such as Friedrich Solmsen, David Sedley, and Culbert Rutenber, who do in fact offer detailed textual analysis of passages in Plato that illustrate his view of God but do not show very much, if any, familiarity with process theism or with neoclassical metaphysics, despite the fact that their results are generally supportive of the views of the process thinkers. There is an obvious need to get these two groups together in that each could benefit from the other.

Leonard Brandwood has performed a valuable service for Plato scholars by collating in one place all of the evidence gathered over the centuries in favor of the thesis that there are stages in Plato's career: internal evidence in the dialogues themselves, external sources such as Aristotle, philological evidence, conceptual evidence of development of certain ideas in Plato's writings, and so on.[20] Of course this general acceptance of the claim that there are stages in Plato's philosophic career is not universal. We will see in the course of the book, however, that even if the thesis that there are *stages* in Plato's career is rejected,[21] there are, at the very least, *facets* to his thought on God that are both clearly distinguishable and worthy of our consideration.

In brief, the picture that results is one where Plato's early dialogues frankly memorialize Socrates and are presumably meant to give us an accurate representation of Socrates' own views. For example, in the *Apology* Plato could hardly have misrepresented Socrates' views in that hundreds of witnesses would still have been alive at the time the *Apology* appeared, as Popper, among others, has emphasized. In the middle dialogues, however, the character Socrates does not necessarily speak for the historical Socrates, especially because the theory of forms developed in this period is not necessarily Socrates' own, in that such a theory is at odds with Socrates' professed ignorance, but rather seems more due to Plato's standpoint. And in the later dialogues this theory of forms is criticized and modified as the character Socrates is given diminished attention, to the point where he vanishes altogether in the *Laws*. Hartshorne's aforementioned chronology very roughly corresponds to Brandwood's, despite the fact that the former sees both significant continuity between the Socratic dialogues and the *Republic* and a significant distinction between the *Parmenides* and the remainder of the late dialogues.

In any event, the present book often mentions, but it does not examine in detail, the early and middle dialogues. That is, the Platonic philosophy of religion I will be exploring concentrates on the late dialogues where, I allege, Plato's most insightful contributions to contemporary philosophy of religion can be found. I should note that the interpreters of Plato with whom I am most concerned in this book (both process interpreters such as Whitehead, Hartshorne, Eslick, and others, as well as nonprocess interpreters such as Sedley, Solmsen, Rutenber, and others) share two assumptions. They all work on the assumptions both that there are stages in Plato's career and that the later dialogues show evidence of trying to improve on the ideas found in the early and middle dialogues, whereas in the early and middle dialogues there is obviously no evidence regarding the subtleties contained in the late dialogues. This is what is meant by asymmetricality.

My concentration on Plato's late dialogues has several practical consequences. I will not be treating in any detail either the *Euthyphro* or the issue of divine command ethics, which have been ably examined by others. Nor will I be saying very much about the topic of immortality (or transmigration) in the *Phaedo* and other dialogues. Once again, this topic has received numerous analyses in the past, and there is no need to reiterate the scholarly work of others, although I must admit that my decision to leave this topic by the wayside is, in part, also influenced by my belief that subjective immortality is not as crucial to religious belief as many assume it to be.[22] Likewise, I will not spend much time on Plato's concessions to popular piety or to the phenomena of the popular religion of his day. Various classicists have already picked these topics clean.

Several recent studies of Socrates' own piety, his prayers, and the relationship between reason and religion in his thought will also be largely ignored.[23] This avoidance should not be interpreted as a denigration of either Socrates or his interpreters but rather as an acknowledgment of the need for an intellectual division of labor concerning Plato's difficult texts. I will be concentrating on a *Platonic* philosophy of religion, leaving the fascinating question of Socrates and the divine for others, including the well-known texts on love in the *Symposium* and *Phaedrus*, as well as the treatments of religious enthusiasm or madness in the *Ion* and *Phaedrus*. Finally, I will also be avoiding both the problem of recollection in Plato and the various meanings of *eternity* in the *Timaeus* and elsewhere.

My hope is that by being clear regarding what I will not treat I will both prevent false expectations in my readers and alert them early on regarding what the book is really about.

PLATO'S WRITINGS

A related scholarly concern surrounds the relationship between Plato's dialogues and Plato's own thoughts. In the present book I will not adopt the view that has become increasingly popular in recent years (although it is still, I think, a minority view) that Plato never lets his own thoughts be articulated in the dialogues, or at least that we should be skittish about talking in terms of "Plato's philosophy." Despite the helpful admonition to treat Plato's dialogues *as dialogues*, the careful defenses of this approach to Plato do not convince me.[24] It must be admitted that in a famous passage in the presumably autobiographical *Seventh Letter* (341C) Plato indicates the unsuitability of propositional language for the expression of philosophic knowledge.[25] But this apophatic moment in Plato's thought, common to almost every major figure in the history of religion, is perfectly compatible with a more general kataphatic approach. That is, Plato *says* a great deal, not only in the *Seventh Letter*, but also in his dialogues through certain characters who are his presumed mouthpieces. Why did he write these latter if not to use them so as to asymptotically approach the truth and to lead others to do the same?

Kenneth Sayre is helpful in the effort to show how, despite all of the blind alleys and apparent contradictions in Plato's dialogues, there is a sort of direction and purpose in evidence: *elenchus* prepares the ground, the use of examples sows the seeds, dialectic trains the shoots, and the "final vision" (discussed in chapter 6 of the present book) allows us to reap the fruits of the philosophic life, to use Sayre's helpful metaphors.[26]

It should be emphasized that the title of the present book is not *Plato's Philosophy of Religion*, but rather *A Platonic Philosophy of Religion*. That is, if my assumptions are false that there are *stages* in Plato's philosophic career and that the later stages can improve on the earlier ones, but not vice versa (hence the asymmetricality of the dialogues), then there are still different *facets* of his philosophy that can be used to construct a philosophy of religion that is quite thought provoking. Likewise, if my assumption is false that Plato speaks through certain characters in his dialogues, there are nonetheless very interesting positions regarding God that are voiced in the dialogues that deserve a hearing even if the voice is (quite incredibly!) not Plato's. Although the dialogues certainly do not present a coherent system, one can nonetheless extrapolate a cosmology or a metaphysics in a systematic way from them, as Patricia Cook notices in her treatment of Neville's use of Plato.[27]

The beliefs in the asymmetricality of the dialogues and in the Platonic voice in the dialogues are loosely connected. I assume that in the early dialogues Plato is memorializing Socrates, hence the character Socrates speaks for himself in these dialogues. In the middle dialogues, however, it is questionable if the character Socrates speaks for himself. It seems far more likely that he speaks for Plato, especially regarding the theory of forms. And in the later dialogues the preferred view (the Platonic view) is often presented through characters other than Socrates: the Eleatic Stranger in the *Sophist*, the Athenian in the *Laws*, and so on. In any event, regarding both of these problems the scholarship on Plato that I will offer is intended to help illuminate not only Plato's own views but also issues in contemporary philosophy of religion. The reader will notice that I would prefer, like the crying child of the *Sophist* (249D), to have both at once: accurate Plato scholarship and a defensible, contemporary, Platonic philosophy of religion.

I readily admit that the present book will not solve several scholarly debates in Plato scholarship regarding possible unity in the Platonic corpus,[28] the stages in Plato's philosophic career, and the presence or absence of Plato's voice in the dialogues, for example, but, once again, my assumptions regarding these matters are at least on the table here in the introduction before I get about the prime business of the book in chapter 1. One final comment in this regard may be needed, however, along the lines defended by Richard Kraut:

> Plato's works were not written to be entered into competition and performed at civic religious festivals, as were the plays of the Greek tragedians and comedians. Plato is not assigning lines to his speakers in order to win a competition or to compose a work that will be considered beautiful or emotionally satisfying by official judges or an immense audience. The dramatist does have this aim, and if it suits his purpose to have his main characters express views that differ from his own, he will do so. But if Plato's aim in writing is to create an instrument that can, if properly used, guide others to the truth and the improvement of their souls, then it may serve his purpose to create a leading speaker who represents the sincere convictions of Plato himself. The point is that, if Plato's aims differ from those of a dramatist, then he will have a reason that the dramatist lacks for using his main speakers as a mouthpiece for his own convictions.[29]

That is, Charles Griswold and others (e.g., David Roochnik) are to be thanked for reminding us that it is possible to underestimate the dramatic content of Plato's dialogues. But as I see things, there is also a danger involved in overestimating such dramatic content.

GOD AND THE GODS

Another preliminary matter that must be addressed is Plato's notorious wavering between the singular and the plural (*theos* and *theoi*, respectively) when talking about the divine, and the related problem of whether to transliterate *theos* as "God" or as "god." Throughout the book I will tend to refer to Plato's concept of God, but by using the singular form, and by capitalizing the first letter, I do not necessarily subscribe to the eighteenth- and nineteenth-century translators' tendency to equate Plato's God with the traditional deity in Christianity. Indeed, as is well known, the whole point to process or neoclassical theism is to criticize this traditional concept (which is often somewhat misleadingly referred to as "classical theism"). Nonetheless, what Plato divined in theory (that theism does not lessen, but rather enhances, an appreciation for change and for the myriad qualities of transient experience) some process thinkers claim is revealed in act in an incarnational religion such as Christianity.

Likewise, by referring to a Platonic *philosophy of religion* I am nonetheless aware of the fact that this branch of philosophy was never explicitly seen as such until late modern thinkers such as Kant and Hegel came on the scene.[30] That is, by "a Platonic philosophy of religion" I merely intend a disciplined rational account of the existence and nature of God on the basis of the evidence supplied in Plato's writings. I do not intend the specific intellectual baggage regarding religion found, say, in Kant or Hegel.

It is no secret that previous scholarly disagreements regarding Plato's concept(s) of '*theos*'/'*theoi*' were often due to conscious or unconscious importation of Victorian religiosity, Nietzschean atheism, Ivy League or Oxbridge agnosticism, and so on. For example, P. E. More, who abhorred pantheism, rejected the claim that Plato's World Soul was God primarily due to the belief that if the World Soul were God, then Plato would be a pantheist. We will see, however, that pantheism does not exhaust the possible modes of divine world inclusiveness if pan*en*theism is intelligible. I am not claiming that I have the ability to see Plato in a completely unbiased fashion. What I am holding is that previous biases have prevented most commentators from seeing certain things in Plato's thoughts on God that are most instructive.

A debate between A. E. Taylor and F. M. Cornford in the 1930s sums up well the difficulty here. Overemphasizing either Plato's monotheism or his polytheism can lead to problems regarding the texts that one has to suppress. Although Taylor and Cornford reached rapprochement on this issue, Taylor had a greater tendency to view Plato as a monotheist, whereas Cornford could not completely relinquish belief in Plato as a polytheist. But if Plato's lesser gods, seen as concessions to popular piety, are all under the sovereignty of a unified will and intelligence, then ultimately monotheism is implied in Plato's God as the soul for the body of the whole world (the World Soul). As William Lane Craig puts the point, "To allow Plato to speak of God (with the capital letter) is to run much less risk of falsifying his thought than to call him a pagan polytheist."[31]

Some scholars will no doubt continue to emphasize Plato's gods due to the fact that Plato never completely abandons the gods of ancient Greek tradition. I have no quarrel with this scholarly tendency as long as it is realized both that Platonic polytheism, to the extent that there is such, can only be understood against the background of Plato's metaphysics and his cosmological monism and that Plato's metaphysics and cosmology were parts of a continuous process of adapting and transforming the orthodoxy of his day.[32]

THE PLAN OF THE BOOK

The book has six chapters, which are arranged in what I hope is an intelligible order. Chapter 1 is titled "Taking the World Soul Seriously." In this chapter

I examine Plato's cosmological monism and his commitment to what is later called "divine omnipresence." The ubiquity of deity in a Platonic cosmos has implications for several key issues surrounding divine embodiment, the contemporary revolt against dualism, the compatibility between seeing God as the World Soul and some version of monotheism (if not the traditional version of monotheism in Judaism, Christianity, and Islam), and so on. Because of these implications, this first chapter is crucial for understanding the remainder of the book. In this chapter I react primarily to the interpretation of Richard Mohr. My own stance is informed first by Hartshorne's metaphysics but then by the work of the classicist Friedrich Solmsen.

Chapter 2 deals with the most sophisticated definition of "being" in Plato's corpus, that found in the *Sophist* (247E) to the effect that being is *dynamis* or dynamic power. The title of this chapter, "Being *Is* Power," indicates the importance of this definition in that if being just *is* the power to affect, or to be affected by, others, then God's power could not, for metaphysical reasons, be so extensive so as to be omnipotent. Various critics are considered from several different philosophical "camps," with Hartshorne and Whitehead supplying the main intellectual insights for the basically Platonic critique of divine omnipotence that I offer.

In chapter 3, titled "Forms as Items in Divine Psychical Process," I explore the relationship between God and the forms, a relationship that is obviously important in any philosophy of religion that is Platonic. On the view I defend, which I think is implied in Plato even if it is not made explicit, the forms are ideas in the divine mind, as the Neoplatonists alleged. The divine mind is characterized by omniscience, to use a term that comes into prominence after the time of Plato. This view removes what is a stumbling block for many readers of Plato regarding what is otherwise the free-floating ontological status of the forms. That is, Plato himself was not necessarily a "Platonist" *if* what it means to be a Platonist is to believe in universals that are not located in the thinking process of some (supremely adequate) knower.[33]

The focus in chapter 4 is on Plato's dipolar theism, a term borrowed from process thinkers such as Hartshorne and Eslick. Here I will correct the standard mistake of confusing Plato's dipolar categorical scheme (being versus becoming, etc.) with his cosmological monism; conversely, Aristotle defended a monopolar categorical scheme of embodied form, yet he ended up with a cosmological dualism more severe than anything found in Plato's dialogues. In this chapter I provide my main argument against the charge that Plato's theism is a type of ontolatry, a worship of being in contrast to becoming. The influence of Plato's alleged ontolatry on the history of philosophical theology, however, has been enormous.

Chapter 5 is titled "Arguments for the Existence of God." Plato, like contemporary religious believers who are philosophers, faces the problem of trying to figure out how to respond intellectually to atheists (and agnostics). In Plato there is an implied version of the ontological argument in the *Republic* (as detailed by J. Prescott Johnson) as well as explicit versions of the cosmological argument in the *Timaeus* and *Laws* (as detailed by William Lane Craig). These versions of the cosmological argument are mixed in with a version of the teleological argument. Hartshorne's most important distinction between the abstract *existence* of God (the fact that God exists) and the contingent *actuality* of God (how God exists or the mode of divine existence) is the focus of this chapter in that this distinction is needed in order to show how the necessary existence of God is compatible with the dynamic actuality of God as the World Soul.

The final chapter of the book is titled "Becoming like God." It deals, in particular, with passages in the *Theaetetus* and *Timaeus* that suggest that the goal of a human life is to become like God to the extent possible (*homoiosis theoi kata to dynaton*). Here I will rely to a great extent on Sedley and Rutenber in their explications of these passages. In general, however, this chapter deals with Platonic mysticism or with experience of God in Plato's dialogues. The goal here will be to rescue Plato's theory from the charge of being overly intellectual in that his theism also provides room (not provided by a God who is an Aristotelian unmoved mover) for inter-action between a human being and God.

I would like to point out that none of the six chapters in the book deals exclusively, or even primarily, with Platonic theodicy. It would be incorrect to conclude from this, however, that the topic of theodicy is peripheral to my central concern. Nothing could be further from the truth. *Every* chapter discusses Platonic theodicy at some point, such that my views on this topic develop gradually throughout the book.

Several translations of Plato's dialogues have been consulted. However, unless otherwise noted, I will be citing the translations conveniently gathered in the Hamilton-Cairns edition of the dialogues and letters. I have followed throughout the Greek edition of Burnet. When citing Greek words I have transliterated the Greek alphabet into our own on the assumption that a greater number of readers will benefit from this procedure. Those who know Greek can easily check the Burnet edition to look for accents, rough breathings, and so on.

Chapter One

Taking the World Soul Seriously

INTRODUCTION

Does God have a body? Religious traditionalists in the Abrahamic religions (Judaism, Christianity, Islam) have had a tendency to answer this question in the negative. But the contemporary revolt against dualism (to use A. O. Lovejoy's phrase) requires us to examine this question carefully in that to deny that God has a body seems to commit a religious believer to a cosmological dualism wherein God (as pure spirit) transcends the natural world altogether. The problem here is that we, like other animals, come into contact with the rest of the world through our bodies, hence a belief in cosmological dualism makes God's awareness of the world radically different from, not even remotely analogous to, our awareness of it.

In this chapter I will examine Plato's cosmological monism (not cosmological dualism!) wherein God is viewed as the mind or soul for the body of the whole natural world, as the World Mind or World Soul. For over sixty-five years Hartshorne tried to explicate and defend this Platonic mind-body relation on a theological level. Briefly, the claim is that whereas our animal bodies are fragments of the cosmos, the divine animal's body *is* the cosmos.

One of the attractions of this view from the perspective of the Abrahamic religions is the intimacy between a conscious subject and its own body, an intimacy that is far greater than that implied in the familiar theological analogy between parent (especially male parent) and child. When Whitehead famously referred to God as "the fellow sufferer who understands," he could have noted that this understanding applies best to the relationship one has to one's own bodily cells (or to one's nerves—*neura*—for the ancient Greeks).[1]

In addition to the intimacy of the World Soul with respect to the body of the world, wherein God is closer than breathing and nearer than hands or feet, there is the ease with which one can account for the ubiquity of deity, a ubiquity that is quite a puzzle in any sort of cosmological dualism. On the World Soul doctrine, although there is no external environment for God, there is an internal one where it is possible for God to really care for, or sympathize with, the creatures.[2]

PROBLEMS WITH MOHR'S ANALYSIS

Richard Mohr, one of the most recent in-depth commentators on Plato's cosmology, is probably not alone in his claim that Plato's World Soul is the oddest of many odd components in Plato's cosmology in that it is highly counterintuitive. Most of the world, according to Mohr, "just does not feel like an animal. Most of it is clearly inert."[3] But *is* this clear, as Mohr alleges? Further, according to Mohr, the World Soul is either redundant (if the World Soul is merely one more autokinetic soul, then it has no special function in Plato's cosmology) or useless (if the World Soul crafts external objects, then it becomes indistinguishable from the Demiurge).

Mohr realizes that the World Soul is an important doctrine for Plato, as is evidenced by the fact that it appears in four (actually five, including *Epinomis*) of the later dialogues (*Statesman, Philebus, Timaeus, Laws*).[4] But if the body of the whole universe is alive and possesses a single World Soul it is an "odd-sounding creature" in need of contemporary explication. The purpose of this chapter is to offer such an explication, to make the World Soul not only an intelligible concept but also to *defend* belief in the World Soul such that one need not exhibit Mohrlike reticence in taking Plato's World Soul seriously.

In this explication and defense I will rely on two thinkers who offer different modes of appreciating the World Soul: Hartshorne (who explicitly defends belief in the World Soul through a reliance on various principles fundamental to his process or neoclassical philosophy of religion) and Friedrich Solmsen (who places the World Soul within the context of Plato's philosophy of religion, in particular, and within Plato's entire philosophy).

Although I am not familiar with any contemporary analytic philosophers who can be used to defend belief in the World Soul, it should be noted that Richard Swinburne has defended a much stronger notion of divine embodiment than most theists who are analytic philosophers and that he somewhat bridges the gap between a supernatural God and the divine, cosmic animal.[5]

My hope is that the approaches mentioned above by Hartshorne and Solmsen will, like the strands in a Peircian cable, mutually reinforce each other in the explication and defense of the World Soul. Before moving to these two thinkers, however, it will be helpful to make clear why there is a need to consult them in order to understand and appreciate the importance of the World Soul.

Mohr's response to the supposed oddness of the World Soul consists in an attenuated version of the concept whereby the World Soul is disassociated from the autokinesis of soul found in the *Phaedrus* and *Laws* X and from any cosmological function other than the mere maintainance of an already established order.

Mohr notes that in the *Statesman* (269C–D) the universe is described by the Eleatic Stranger (and presumably by Plato) as a living creature (*zoon*) endowed with reason (*phronesin*). But he is premature in divorcing the World Soul from self-motion. When the Stranger says that we must not claim that the universe moves itself, he seems to be denying that it could go anywhere in that the World Soul animates the whole body of the world; there is no place for it to go. Later in the same speech (270A), however, the Stranger makes it clear that when the Demiurge withdraws from the world the soul of the world must move by its own innate force. That is, the World Soul must take control of the affairs of the universe when God (Cronus or the Demiurge) "withdraws" (274A), a comparison that I will later emphasize. Because there is no denial of autokinesis to the World Soul, the definition of soul as self-motion in the *Phaedrus* and *Laws* X would seem to apply to the World Soul as well as to the human soul.

The comparison between a human being and the World Soul is *noticed* by Mohr in his treatment of the World Soul in the *Philebus* (30A–B), but it is not used, as it is in Hartshorne, to make intelligible to modern readers why Plato believes in the World Soul, why Plato sees the World Soul as a cause, and why the besouled (*empsychon*) body of the world is fairer (*kalliona*) than our bodies.

Despite numerous clues in the *Timaeus* as to how to ameliorate the oddness of the World Soul, Mohr concentrates on the "parallel structures and synchronized motions" between the World Soul and the world body. That is, he does not seem to see them as integrally connected in such a way that the World Soul animates the body of the world. Timaeus (and presumably Plato) makes it clear (30A) that God desired that all things should be good, to the extent that this is possible (*bouletheis gar ho theos agatha men panta, phlauron de meden einai kata dynamin*), by intelligently creating order out of disorder (*eis taxin auto egagen ek tes ataxias*). But divine intelligence, it is equally clear (30B), *presupposes* soul. Mohr does not emphasize this. In fact, the world "came into being" when God put intelligence into the soul of the bodily world—a living creature (*ton kosmon zoon empsychon ennoun te te aletheia dia ten tou theou genesthai pronoian*).

The world is made in the likeness of an animal (*zoon*), or better, the individual animals in the world are parts of the whole animal. That is, the World Soul is the original animal (30C). The need for the World Soul becomes apparent when Plato comes to the realization that there is only one world (31A), literally a uni-verse. If there were two worlds there would be a need for a more comprehensive being to include both. The fact that the World Soul is called the "solitary, perfect" animal (*monosin homoion e to pantelei zooi*) is an invitation, refused by Mohr, to think through what Hartshorne has called the "logic of perfection."

Because divine intelligence presupposes the World Soul (30B), and because divine intelligence is either eternal (outside of time altogether) or everlasting (existing throughout all of time), it should not surprise us that the world is not liable to old age or disease (33A) in that it must be eternal (or better, everlasting), too. Further (33C), there is no need to push the animal body comparison so far as to claim that the world has eyes because there is nothing outside of itself to be seen; nor is there any need for ears to hear any being external to it; lungs are not needed to take in air from without in that there is no "without" to the all-inclusive organism; and a digestive system is not needed if there is no external source of nourishment that must be tapped in order for the World Soul to survive. The excellence of the World Soul/world body complex consists largely, but not exclusively, as we will see, in its self-sufficiency (33D—*autarkes*). The absence of external enemies eliminates the need for hands for defense (34A), and as we have seen, there is no possibility for the world to move to another place because it is its own place. There may well be other sorts of motion, however, contra Mohr, of which the World Soul is capable.

At 34B three significant points are made that militate against Mohr's truncated version of the World Soul: (a) The World Soul is diffused throughout the body of the world (*psychen de eis meson autou theis dia pantos te eteinen kai eti exothen to soma aute periekalypsen*) and hence does not have a mere parallel or epiphenomenal structure with relation to the body of the world, as Mohr alleges. (b) The World Soul is not to be divorced from God in that it is itself "generated" by the Demiurge as a blessed God (*dia panta de tauta eudaimona theon auton egennesato*). In order to understand the World Soul, one must therefore explain how the Demiurge and the World Soul are both divine, which Hartshorne tries to do. And (c), Timaeus makes it clear that the soul was not made after the body. In fact, because the universe is eternal or everlasting (37D), and because the body of the world cannot antedate the World Soul, the World Soul must also be eternal or everlasting such that the independence of the Demiurge from the World Soul cannot be literally construed as temporal priority. (Also see 34B–37A, 92C.)

Further, I am not sure what Mohr means when he criticizes various commentators on the *Timaeus* (Cornford, Cherniss, Archer-Hind, Herter, and Rosen) by saying that they offer "(unneeded) charitable attempts to dismiss Plato's thought from Christian thought and more generally as attempts to reduce the number of unfashionable theological commitments in Plato's cosmology." Is Mohr agreeing with Plato's theological commitments or disagreeing with them? Or more likely, is Mohr saying that we should not even try to link up Plato's view of God with contemporary philosophical theology?[6]

Mohr does not treat Plato's use of the World Soul in the *Laws*, perhaps because of his belief that the World Soul does not possess self-motion, and *Laws* X is the prime text where self-motion is treated. The Athenian (presumably Plato) makes it clear that self-movement is the *definition* of soul (896A—*ten dynamenen auten hauten kinean kinesin*), which implies that *all* soul possesses this property or it would not be soul. Soul is the *universal* cause of all change and motion (*epeide ge anephane metaboles te kai kineseos hapases aitia hapasin*). That is, a soulless body would have to be moved by something else (896B). Soul is (metaphysically) prior to body (896C—*psychen men proteran gegonenai somatos hemin, soma de deuteron te kai hysteron, psyches archouses, archomenon kata physin*) and controls all things universally (896D—*psychen de diokousan kai enoikousan en hapasin tois pante kinoumenois mon*).

Plato's theodicy is a difficult topic, as we will see. It is worth noting here, however, that Plato sees the universe as being guided in wisdom by a supremely good soul (897C—*delon hos ten aristen psychen phateon epimeleisthai tou kosmou pantos kai agein auton ten toiauten hodon ekeinen*). The soul by which the circle of the heavens turns is supremely good (898C—*aristen psychen*). As before, these claims are seemingly irresistible invitations, nonetheless resisted by Mohr, to think through the relationships among the World Soul, the logic of perfection, and divinity. Hartshorne warmly receives such invitations. (Also see 902E, 903E–905E, 967C; and *Epinomis* 981B, 982B, 983C.)[7]

HARTSHORNE'S DEFENSE OF THE WORLD SOUL

Process theology in general can be regarded as a partial return to Plato because of his World Soul as the divine self-moved, but not unmoved, mover of all other self-movers and as the soul aware of all things. To help explicate Hartshorne's views on the World Soul, three sorts of psyche (P) can be distinguished, all three of which can be found in Plato and Hartshorne in various ways under different labels. P1 is psyche at the microscopic level of cells, atomic particles, and the like, where contemporary physics has vindicated Plato's flirtation with panpsychism, as in the passages from the *Laws* cited in the previous section. (Although the Greeks did not know about cells or subatomic particles, they did speculate about nerves—*neura*.[8]) The nightmare of determinism has faded as reality in its fundamental constituents itself seems to have at least a partially indeterminate character of self-motion. That is, the sum total of efficient causes from the past does not supply the sufficient cause to explain the behavior of the smallest units of becoming in the world. Plato was wiser than he knew; little did he know that in twentieth-century physics universal mechanism would give way to a cosmic dance.

P2 is psyche per se, psyche in the sense of feeling found in animals and human beings, whereby beings with central nervous systems feel as wholes just as their constituent parts prefigure feeling at a local level. And feeling *is* localized. Think of a knife stuck in the gut of any vertebrate or of sexual pleasure. P2 consists in taking these local feelings and collecting them so that an individual as a whole can feel what happens to its parts, even if the individual partially transcends the parts.

In the *Republic* (462C–D) Plato makes it clear (through the character Socrates) that if there is pain in one's finger (note, not the whole hand) the entire community (*pasa he koinonia*) of bodily connections is hurt; the organized unity of the individual is such that when one part is hurt there is a feeling of pain in the human being as a whole (*hole*) who has the pain in her finger.[9]

P3 is divine psyche. If I am not mistaken, Plato shares with Hartshorne the following four-term analogy: P1 : P2 :: P2 : P3. The universe is a society or an organism (a Platonic World Soul) of which one member (the Platonic Demiurge) is preeminent just as human beings or animals are societies of cells (or nerves) of which the mental part is preeminent.

Because animal individuals must, to maintain their integrity, adapt to their environments, mortality is implied. But if we imagine the World Soul we must not consider an environment external to deity but an internal one: the world body of the World Mind (the Demiurge) or the World Soul. This cosmic, divine animal has such an intimate relation to its body that it must also have ideal ways of perceiving and remembering its body such that it can identify the microindividuals (P2) it includes. We can only tell when cells in our toe have been burned by the fire; we cannot identify the microindividuals (P1) as such.[10]

It is true that there are several different plausible interpretations of the relationship between the Demiurge and the orderliness of the world. One such view is that the Demiurge is hampered by the inherent disorderliness in the realm of necessity (*anangke*) in the effort to conform the world or the contents of the receptacle to the ideal. Hartshorne does not so much reject this view as supplement it with the claim that the Demiurge is also impeded by a plurality of self-movers. The value of contrast and richness provided by "cosmic creativity" also provides the "recalcitrance of the material," just as there is the "familiar difficulty of eliciting harmony among a plurality of creatures each having its own freedom." Although the evidence from Plato is somewhat unclear as to how matter "could consist of multitudinous souls of extremely subhuman kinds," and as to how the order of the universe could be a static good forever (which Hartshorne thinks is impossible), he had at least a glimmering "that it was the multiplicity of souls that made absolute order impossible."[11]

On Hartshorne's view philosophers have often myopically focused on the Plato they could understand and ignored the Plato who was too profound for them. This is most evident with respect to Plato's panentheistic conception of the divine soul for the world. (*Panentheism* literally means that all is *in* God.) But Hartshorne has taken the World Soul as a clue for present philosophizing. For example, each new divine state harmonizes itself both with its predecessor and with the previous state of the cosmos. This is analogous to a human being harmonizing itself with its previous experience and bodily state, but with a decisive difference. The human being must hope that its internal environment and the external environment will continue to make it possible for it to survive, whereas God has no such problem in that there is no external environment for God.[12] But the differences between God and human beings (e.g., God knows the microindividuals included in the divine life, and God has no external environment) should not cloud the important similarities (e.g., the facts that self-change is integral to soul at all levels and that the soul-body analogy used to understand God does not preclude the person-person analogy, which links the divine person with human beings). The most important similarity lies in the fact that one's bodily cells are associated, at a given moment, with one as a conscious, supercellular singular, just as all lesser beings are associated with the society of singulars called "God."[13] In a way, all talk about God short of univocity contains *some* negativity, in that God does not exist, know, love, and so on, as we do. With regard to the divine body, however, many theists have allowed this negativity to run wild.[14] Hartshorne's use of Plato is an attempt to remedy this imbalance.

Plato offered a "striking anticipation" of the doctrine of the compound individual, even if he ultimately fell short of the principle that individuality as such must be the compounding of organisms into organisms. But this is not surprising because cells were not yet discovered, even if "nerves" were.[15] In the case of the divine individual, where all entities are experienced, there can be no envy of others in that they are internal to the divine goodness. Less completely are a human being's cells internal to the individual; for example, bone cells in one's arm are less internal and less fully possessed by the individual than are the brain cells. These conditions regarding divine inclusiveness also explain why the cosmos could not be held together and ordered by a malevolent God or by a plurality of gods (as hypothesized by Hume), in that these deities are always partly divided within or among themselves and are incapable of an objective grasp of the forms. The cosmos can be held together only by an all-sympathetic coordinator.[16]

Plato also came closer than any other philosopher to Hartshorne's notion that God is *whole* in "every categorical sense, all actuality in one individual actuality, and all possibility in one individual potentiality," albeit tempered by Hartshorne's own understanding of the potentiality inherent in God, somewhat different from that found in Whitehead's view. And because of this wholeness God is not an organism of a loose kind who must await the light years it takes for cosmic interactions to take place because these interactions are all internal to the divine "ideal animal" itself.[17]

One of the reasons why Hartshorne thinks of Plato as among the "wisest and best" of theologians is that he thinks Plato may have realized that the Demiurge *is* the World Soul in abstraction; that is, the Demiurge is that part of the World Soul that is forever engaged in realizing eternal or everlasting ideals. (It must be admitted, however, that here more than elsewhere Hartshorne is interpreting Plato rather loosely for the purpose of present philosophizing. The connection he draws between the Demiurge and the World Soul is much closer than anything stated explicitly in the *Timaeus*.) This process of realization is what Plato means in the *Timaeus* by the "moving image of eternity." Hartshorne's tempting way of reading Plato alleges that God, utilizing partly self-created creatures, "creates its own forever unfinished actualization." Thus, God is aware of both us and other non-cosmic animals and the lesser souls, on the one hand, and eternal ideals, on the other. Even though God is the "individual integrity" of the world, which is otherwise a concatenation of myriad parts, Hartshorne's view is easily made compatible with the claim that God does not survey all events in the future with strict omniscience.[18]

Belief in a World Soul as the divine animal is connected with a belief in a world body, which is superior to our bodies because there is nothing internal to it (e.g., cancer cells) that could threaten its continued existence, even if the divine body happens to be spatially finite. Further, our bodies are fragmentary, as in a human infant's coming into the world as a secondary being expressing its feelings upon a system that already has a basic order in its cells; whereas the divine body does not begin to exist on a foundation otherwise established. When an animal dies, its individual lifestyle no longer controls its members, yet the result is not chaos but "simply a return to the more pervasive types of order expressive of the cosmic mind-body." The World Soul is aware of the divine body and can vicariously suffer with its suffering members, but it cannot suffer in the sense of ceasing to exist due to an alien force. "An individual can influence it, none can threaten it." Not even brain death can threaten it because the soul-body analogy cannot be pushed to the point where a divine brain is posited. As before, the contrast between the brain and a less essential bodily part only makes sense because an animal has an external environment. Consider again that the divine body does not need limbs to move about, for it is its own place: "space being merely the order among its parts." It does not need a digestive system or lungs to take in food or air from without in that there is no "without." So it is with all organs outside the central nervous system, which, as we know but Plato did not, is the organ that adapts "internal activities to external stimuli," a function that is not needed in the inclusive organism. The prime function of the divine body is to furnish the World Soul with awareness of, and power over, its bodily members. So although there is no special part of the cosmos recognizable as a nervous system, every individual becomes, *as it were*, a brain cell directly communicating to the World Soul and likewise receiving influences from divine feeling or thought.[19]

SOLMSEN AND PLATO'S THEOLOGY

Hartshorne's favorable treatment of the World Soul is both an attempt to make intelligible to modern readers some rather difficult texts in Plato on the World Soul and an attempt (largely successful, I think) to suggest why belief in a World Soul is superior to disbelief in God, belief in pantheism, or belief in God as a strictly transcendent, supernatural, purely eternal, unmoved mover. Solmsen's project, which supplements Hartshorne's, is to concentrate on Plato, to locate the World Soul within the context of Plato's theology as it developed throughout his career.[20] I would like to show why Solmsen's work

is one of the best on Plato's thoughts on God to date. That is, Solmsen is able
to show why the World Soul is a central element in Plato's theology, something that is not done by most subsequent commentators on Plato.

Solmsen makes it clear that the background to Plato's theology is provided by a traditional view of civic religion whereby piety of a nonpolitical
sort or a purely secular patriotism would have been contradictions in terms.
The destruction of the old religion had both a positive and a negative effect:
it both made it possible for a more sophisticated, intellectual conception of
God, and it opened the door to atheism. Plato meant to close this door and
to elevate religious discourse. This elevation would, given Plato's lifelong
interest in politics, have to be able to establish some sort of rapprochement
with civic religion even if the primitive identification of the interests of the
polis with a particular deity would have to be dropped. Further, this elevation would have to continue the pioneering work of the Pre-Socratics,
whose objective was to connect the deity (or deities) to cosmic processes in
nature, a connection that very often led to belief in the World Soul.

Solmsen details how Xenophanes and Aeschylus partially prepared the
way for Plato by indicating that God (Plato's Demiurge) was a mind who
acted without physical effort; Euripides at times thought of God in cosmic
terms; Anaxagoras and Diogenes of Apollonia dealt with an intelligent organ-
izer of the world—anything that serves its purpose well as a bodily organ cannot be the work of luck (*tyche*). This groping for a cosmic deity as opposed
to a political one was characteristic of several Pre-Socratic thinkers. A philosophical "science" was taking over the lead in the search for a new divine principle. This concept of God as cosmic was not threatened by political
upheaval, and hence philosophy of nature was the chief potential source for
new religious beliefs. Plato criticized the traditional gods in the construction
of the Republic so as to make room for the World Soul/Demiurge in the
Timaeus, as the beginning of this latter dialogue indicates.[21]

Other scholars indicate how in Empedocles the cosmic sphere was given
a divine status and how Thales, Anaximenes, and the Pythagoreans believed
in a World Soul. Further, there is a contrast between human learning of many
things (*polymathia*), on the one hand, and the divine wisdom of the World
Soul, on the other, a wisdom that is found in several forms in Heraclitus: *hen
to sophon*, universal logos, cosmic *gnome*, and *kyberman panta*. The very idea
of a cosmos leads to a belief in the cosmic God, the contemplation of which
largely constitutes human wisdom; we are constituents of cosmic order.
Heraclitus sometimes personified the cosmic principle as Zeus and at other
times viewed it as a rarefied, all-pervading presence, like ether, a view that was
later made famous by the Stoics.[22]

In fact, according to Plutarch, all of the ancient philosophers, except Aristotle and the atomists, believed that the world was informed with a divine animal soul![23] This is a claim that, even if an exaggeration, nonetheless shows how comfortable the ancients were with the World Soul, a comfort matched by modern discomfort.

Plato's attempt to reform religion is initially seen in the effort to define piety (*eusebeia*) in the *Euthyphro*, a reform that is intensified in the *Republic*. One practical result of this reform was a confrontation with the theodicy problem, which is resolved by Plato by noticing the limits of divine power (limits that are perfect in their own way in that they allow creatures self-motion) and the purity of divine goodness. Nonetheless in the *Republic* the gods (Plato often wavers between the singular and the plural, as we have seen) seem to occupy a plane below the highest. The gods are not inconsistent with the forms in the *Republic*, but their relation is not made clear in this work. Solmsen's tempting way of putting the problem is in the following Aristotelian terms: the forms provide, of course, the formal cause of goodness in the world, yet goodness will never be concretely produced in the world unless there is an efficient (divine) cause, an efficient cause made explicit in later dialogues in divine dipolarity (World Soul/Demiurge).[24]

Further, the *Sophist* exhibits a theory of forms where the stiffness and isolation of the forms are abandoned in favor of dynamic power, as we will see. The preparation for this dynamism is found in the *Phaedrus*'s principle of psyche as self-motion, a principle that makes it possible for the World Soul to be an organic whole, such that neither materialism nor the theory of forms contains the full truth about reality. (F. M. Cornford, contra Mohr, emphasizes that the World Soul as a *zoon* must be self-moved if only because it was a commonplace in antiquity that animals were self-moved.)[25] However, Plato is quite willing, as we have seen, to "materialize" the whole by admitting divine embodiment. While the first part of the *Theaetetus* makes us aware of the dangers of absolutizing movement, these dangers are not necessary if one keeps *dynamis* regulated by form and if one realizes that the dynamic whole is an orderly one, a cosmos. What is to be noted is that almost every one of the late dialogues makes some contribution to the theory of movement, not least of which is the *Timaeus*, where the World Soul is seen as the source of movement,[26] and the *Laws*, where there is an elaborate classification of movements.[27]

Mind (*nous*) contemplates the forms, which are, "in themselves," eternal and immutable abstractions. Hence mind (i.e., the Demiurge) "by itself" lacks the right kind of contact to link up with life and flux. Only soul can do that because soul both animates what would otherwise be the dead body of the world and has, through its mental functioning, communion with the forms.

Perhaps the most insightful commentator on the "amphibious" nature of soul is J. N. Findlay.[28] The World Soul has its feet in both the eidetic and the instantial camps, it is not merely a "link" between these regions; it is a living channel. The eidetic mind works only by way of the World Soul in which it is instantiated. The timeless mind is an "elder" God, in a way, but for Findlay the World Soul fulfills all of the tasks that could be demanded of God, as detailed by Hartshorne in his many writings.

Findlay is also instructive regarding the World Soul in Plotinus, a consideration of which will help us to better understand Plato's view. Here the World Soul is an unquiet faculty (as in Hartshorne's claim that it receives influence from *all* creatures), like Martha busy over many things (*polypragmon*—III.vii.2), in contrast to The One. Hartshorne supplements Findlay's insights. The Greeks—Plato, Aristotle, and Epicurus among them—realized that any possible world must involve a multiplicity of individuals, each making their own decisions. Hence there is an aspect of real chance in what happens. Unfortunately, this notion of chance was not sufficiently synthesized by Plato with the (materialistic) atomism of Leucippus and Democritus or with the "swerve" of atoms (i.e., the tychism) found in Epicurus. It is perhaps this failure that accounts for the monopolarity of the Neoplatonists in their interpretation of Plato, as we will see. In a way, Plotinus reaffirms Plato's "three aspects of the ultimate" in the *Timaeus*: the forms (especially the form of the good), the Demiurge, and the World Soul. These appear in Plotinus, respectively, as The One, Intellect (*nous*), and the Plotinian World Soul.

But Plotinus has a (necessitarian) logical principle for the progression from The One to the World Soul. Plotinus' ontolatry (i.e., his worship of being) differs from Plato's belief in a World Soul because the self-motion of soul in Plato is replaced in Plotinus by a conception of soul with a merely "accidental and superficial motility," a motility derived in an Aristotelian way from body rather than from the soul's own nature. Plotinus at least enhanced Plato's aesthetic argument for God, and he rightly viewed Plato's forms as essentially "objects-for-Nous," but for the most part his monopolarity (i.e., his worship of eminent being to the exclusion of eminent becoming) detracted from an appreciation of Plato's greatest insights regarding the World Soul. Hartshorne finds it "comic" to watch Plotinus trying to prove that without unity and simplicity we cannot understand the multiple and complex. This is correct, but it is equally correct that without plurality, contrast, and complexity there is "no unity, beauty, goodness, value, or reality."[29]

At once Plato's concept of 'soul' preserves the best in the Orphic, Pythagorean, and mystery religion traditions regarding soul; it makes the soul the locus of political virtue; it allows soul to be used to explain the cosmos in religious terms; and, in fact, as we have seen, it even makes mind the auxiliary of soul. The supreme soul, the World Soul, is Plato's attempt to connect the world of flux with that of sameness into an integrated theory of reality. Hence the function of God in the *Timaeus* is not so much to impart life to the universe as to make its life as excellent as possible. The philosophical contemplation of the beauty of the universe (through astronomy and music, where apparently discordant elements are brought into harmony) makes the human soul at least akin to, if not homogeneous with, the Soul of the cosmos.[30]

Two noted scholars whom I do not find helpful in the understanding of the World Soul are P. E. More, who wavered as to whether or not the World Soul was a God, and Gregory Vlastos, who, when the question was asked, "Why does the cosmos have a soul?" responded by saying that the form of a living creature has a soul. In effect, if I understand Vlastos correctly, the main reason why Plato talked about the World Soul was to have a model for the Demiurge to create other (presumably human) souls. But this interpretation fails to take Plato's religiosity seriously, for it implies that the telos of the World Soul is to contribute to us; it is to commit the theological error of putting the human above the divine. I seriously doubt if Plato would have wanted this.[31]

God (the supreme psyche with supreme *nous*) confronts the elements of the world that remain discordant with persuasion (*peitho*), not force (*bia*). But God still has power (*kratos*), specifically the immense power to persuade the world by offering it a model of perfection. Although Solmsen is hesitant to literally identify the Demiurge with the World Soul on the evidence of the *Timaeus*, he is willing to see the two as aspects of one God that deal with separate functions: the World Soul with movement and life and the Demiurge with order, design, and rationality. In the *Laws*, however, such an identification is legitimate. As we have seen, in the *Laws* mind presupposes a living soul, even if mind itself is eternal or everlasting (and even if the Demiurge is mythically depicted as prior to the World Soul in the *Timaeus*).[32]

Solmsen reinforces Hartshorne's notion of a personal deity: once Plato's doctrine of a cosmic soul had taken shape not only did it succeed in "respiritualizing" nature, but it also transformed the indirect relation between the individual and God into a direct and hence personal relationship. The ardor that this relationship fosters constitutes Platonic piety, which, as at the end of the *Euthyphro*, is a type of service (Hartshorne would say contribution) to God.[33]

Paul Friedlander sees this respiritualization of law, art, and nature as the central task of Plato's life. Hence Plato can be said to metaphorically return to Thales' notion that all things are full of gods. Friedlander is also instructive regarding the similarity between the individual and God, for example, in the *Gorgias* (505E). Plato indicates not only that there is a soul for the cosmos but also that there is something like a cosmos or wholeness for the individual soul. That is, the best humans reflect the World Soul in that their common principle is the good (*agathon*). If the world is, as Friedlander notes many contemporary thinkers believe, a mere machine, then the appearance of a leaf or a caterpillar would be "miraculous."[34]

It should not surprise us that in *Laws* X the argument against atheism is described as a prelude (*prooimion*) for the whole body of laws. Religion is the basis of Plato's city here and plays a much more significant role than it did in the *Republic*. It was actually his aim to refute three types of atheism: the denial of God altogether; the belief that divinity does not care for us; and the claim that God can be bought off with sacrifices, and so on. Plato's refutation is in terms of his own theological tenets, including belief in the divine animal. The World Soul in the Laws at times surfaces not as an individual entity (as in the *Timaeus*) but as a generic principle, as some of the texts treated above indicate. Soul does not, however, manifest itself with equal distinctness in every phase of the cosmos; it is in some way intensified in animals, especially in human animals and in the divine animal. But the *constancy* of the world's organic functioning as due to the World Soul is emphasized by Hans-Georg Gadamer, who notices that an animal, even a divine animal, differs from a plant because it can relay back to itself all the stimulations of sense experience. That is, the World Soul integrates the scattered multiplicity of the bodily, an integration that is similar to that found in Anaxagoras and Xenocrates. Gadamer is also helpful in the defense of Hartshorne's version of Platonic theodicy in that the second "bad" World Soul of the *Laws* cannot be taken literally; a second "World" Soul would entail a third to unify the first two into a cosmos, and so on.[35]

As before, the Aristotelian conception of a self-sufficient God who contemplates only itself is entirely alien to Plato. God's *telos*, if there is such, is the best possible harmony for the sum of things: the parts are for the whole, but the whole only flourishes with healthy parts. God is like the good physician who does not give attention to a single, isolated organ, but rather to the body of the world as a whole. Although it would be rash to suggest that Plato felt himself in his later years more at home in the cosmos than in the polis, it must be admitted that he prepared the way (say by his attraction to panpsychism in the *Laws*) for Hellenistic escape from politics into the life of the cosmos.[36] Further, the cosmic scope of the World Soul is, in many ways, a return to the Great Mother tradition in religion that existed before the bifurcation between Father Sky God and Mother Earth Goddess, a bifurcation that gradually tilted heavily toward Father Sky God, out of which Yahweh grew, as Jurgen Moltmann argues.[37]

Solmsen is quite explicit that the "concept of a divine World Soul as the fountain of movements and as the intelligent power controlling the world of Becoming is the cornerstone of the whole new system," a theological system based on physics. Before individual or political experience can be understood, the validity of religion itself has to be understood on cosmic grounds. This understanding makes it possible to consider oneself more of a "citizen of the Universe" than a citizen of any mere political community. Law in a polis is indeed important, but only if it is seen against a larger background, specifically the theological background of the *Timaeus* and *Laws*, which were attempts to stem the process of disintegration in Greek culture that had been in existence for almost a century.[38]

Here we should note that A. E. Taylor is instructive in his belief that the World Soul (God) is far more important in the *Timaeus* than in the *Republic* largely because the World Soul is a key part of a new cosmology without matter (an indirect way of saying that Plato was a panpsychist). Taylor also indicates that the language of God (here the Demiurge) putting soul into the body of the world is obviously not to be taken literally. God (*ariste psyche*) is transcendent and immanent (i.e., dipolar), with the former making it difficult to call Plato's God pantheistic and the latter making it difficult to limit God in an Aristotelian, Thomistic, monopolar way. It is no surprise that Taylor uses Whitehead to criticize monopolarity, as in his criticism of viewing soul at whatever level as "substance."[39]

Plato never abandoned his theory of forms, but the World Soul takes over functions previously fulfilled by the forms. For example, knowledge (*episteme*) and craftsmanship (*techne*) are elevated to positions of great dignity because they either have affinity to soul or are skills that soul itself can attain. God extends control over the region of becoming due to the fact that reason, regularity, order, and form are not limited to the sphere of being (*ta onta*) but can be used by God as values in the harmonization of the world.[40]

THE LEGACY OF THE WORLD SOUL

It is sad that Plato's thoughts on God have been obscured in the history of Platon*ism*. He was the last Greek to discuss God in a context of a political system, and after his death ancient theistic philosophers went in one of two directions: Aristotle moved toward a conception of divinity as transcendent, and the Stoics moved toward pantheism, leaving no one, as it were, to guard the Platonic fort. Solmsen seems to agree with Hartshorne that Christianity has largely followed the Aristotelian move, albeit designated at times as "Platonic," by relying almost exclusively on Plato's form of the good.

The possibility of a genuinely Platonic type of Christianity, wherein the World Soul is taken seriously, is evidenced in Origen. He was a Christian theist who avoided both impersonal pantheism and the view of God as supernatural (cosmological dualism). To briefly sample some of Origen's thoughts in this regard, consider his citation of a question from Jeremiah (23:24), "Do not I fill heaven and earth?, says the Lord," and his use of a famous passage from I Corinthians (12:12), "The body is one and has many members, but all the members, many though they are, are one body, and so it is with Christ." Christ is identified by Origen with an omnipresent logos, with the agape that binds all things together, with the soul for the body of the world.

Or again, Origen is clear that our one body (*corpus nostrum unum*) is composed of many members (*multis membris*) that are held together by one soul (*una anima*). Likewise, the universe is an immense animal of many members that are held together by God (*ita et universum mundum velut animal quoddam immensum atque immane opinandum puto, quod quasi ab una anima virtute Dei*). *Immensum* here entails something vast: the fact that God brings together the world within the boundaries of the divine body.[41]

Perhaps Christians and other theists in the Abrahamic religions should be more sympathetic to the World Soul than they have been to date. If we start with the microcosm, we can then easily understand how cells are brought within the order of our "mesocosmic" bodies. But such an understanding was not always easy. It was not until the early nineteenth century that cell theory took coherent form in the work of Bichat, Muller, Schleiden, Schwann, and Pasteur, work that still has not been assimilated into philosophical theology. It is at least plausible to move to the other side of the mesocosm, where we can see ourselves as parts of a macrocosmic whole.

It must be admitted that Solmsen and Hartshorne, despite the fact that they mutually reinforce each other in the effort to make belief in the World Soul plausible, engage in two quite different types of scholarship. Solmsen is much more interested than Hartshorne in justifying his claims on the basis of evidence from the Platonic texts themselves, but this should not lead us to assume that he was a naive positivist in that he certainly brings his own theoretical baggage to those texts. And Hartshorne is much more interested than Solmsen in doing intellectual work with Plato in the effort to respond to issues in contemporary philosophy of religion, but this should not lead us to assume that Hartshorne is indifferent to the integrity of Plato's texts. Nor is Hartshorne's approach imperialistic in the sense of his wishing to crowd out other interpretations of Plato. Rather, it is *because* he has, in fact, read Plato carefully that he thinks it is appropriate for other scholars to at least take the World Soul seriously as an intellectually respectable position rather than as a piece of antiquarian lore.

Talk about the divine body is not merely a consequence of the use of the soul-body analogy to understand God; it is also logically entailed in Plato's metaphysics, as Hartshorne argues. Hartshorne has often claimed (contra Kant and others) that there are necessary truths concerning existence (e.g., "Something exists"). The absurdity of claiming that "there might have been (absolutely) nothing" is derived from Plato himself, who, when he commits parricide on father Parmenides in the *Sophist* (241–42), only admits the existence of relative nonbeing or otherness, not the existence of absolutely nothing, which would be a logical contradiction in that *it* would then be something. Hartshorne agrees with Plato that all determination is negation, but this inescapable element of negation is precisely Plato's form of otherness or relative nonbeing. The statement *Nothing exists* could not conceivably be verified. That is, a completely restrictive or wholly negative statement is not a conceivable yet unrealized fact but an impossibility. Particular bodies can pass out of existence (or better, pass into another sort of existence), but the divine body of the universe has no alternative but to exist.[42]

My hope is that by taking the World Soul seriously we might (1) eliminate the oddness of this doctrine as it is conceived by many, Mohr among them; (2) make better sense than most commentators (Solmsen excluded) of the movement of Plato's theology in the later dialogues; and (3) learn how to use Plato to respond to several important issues in contemporary philosophy of religion. That is, paradoxical as it may sound, Plato's theology is at once archaic (in that it is an attempt to preserve the best in civic religion, the Great Mother tradition, the mystery cults, and Pre-Socratic religiosity) and future oriented.[43] It is future oriented both because it points toward Hellenistic, cosmic religion and because it provides important clues to show us how to solve some of the unnecessary problems regarding theodicy that have plagued theism for centuries. Plato's theology can also enable us to bridge contemporary philosophical concern for ecology with philosophy of religion but without an appeal to pantheism.

I would like to conclude this chapter with a few remarks on pain that bear on a Platonic theodicy, in particular. The experience of pain in the finger is both mine and something not mine (in that it involves not only my life but the lives of cells, too). Likewise, God can experience our pains without thereby becoming identical with us. This is why "pantheism" should not be seen as exhausting all varieties of divine inclusiveness. "Panentheism" (once again, literally, all is *in* God), as when Plato suggests in the *Timaeus, Laws,* and *Epinomis* that body is in soul, rather than vice-versa, is a type of divine inclusiveness that should no longer be ignored. We are not in God as marbles are in a box or as an idea is in a mind. Rather, if we are to take seriously the Platonic idea of God as the World Soul who animates the body of the world—indeed he refers to it as the "divine animal"—then the sort of panentheistic inclusiveness to be considered is *organic* inclusiveness of bodily pain in a whole animal.[44] It is not without reason that Whitehead traced the origin of his own philosophy of organism back to Plato's *Timaeus,* where, as we will see in the next chapter, it is not so much matter itself that is created but rather a certain sort of order to the natural world that is congenial to our contemporary view wherein there has been a dissolution of material quanta into (partially self-moving) vibrations.[45]

In any event, it is crucial to notice on the evidence in the *Timaeus* that there is only one cosmos (rather than one in an infinite series, as the atomists believed) that is shaped in the image of the form of a living being, a form that is part of the content of the divine mind. Although scholars have been quick to notice the difference between the form of a living being and the perceptual world animal, they have generally not been as quick to notice that while the inclusion of forms in the divine mind is somewhat like the inclusion of contents of thought within any mind, the inclusion of the world in God is actually *organic* inclusiveness, on the analogy of parts included in an animal body.[46] This has implications, as we will see, for understanding the relationship between God (the World Soul) and the evils or pains that exist in the natural world.

Chapter Two

Being *Is* Power

INTRODUCTION

Whereas the previous chapter was intended to shed Platonic light on the divine attribute of omnipresence (and omnibenevolence), the present chapter is intended to shed Platonic light on the unintelligibility of the divine attribute of omnipotence conceived as the monopoly of divine power. Consider the following crucial passage from the Eleatic Stranger (presumably Plato) in the *Sophist* (247E):

> I suggest that anything has real being that is so constituted as to possess any sort of power either to affect anything else or to be affected, in however small a degree, by the most insignificant agent, though it be only once. I am proposing as a mark to distinguish real things that they are nothing but power. (Lego de to kai hopoianoun tine kektemenon dynamin eit eis to poien heteron hotioun pephykos eit eis to pathein kai smikrotaton hypo tou phaulotatou, kan ei monon eis hapax, pan touto ontos einai. Tithemai gar horon horizein ta onta hos estin ouk allo ti plen dynamis.)

The specific purposes of this chapter are to claim (1) that this passage is one of the most important in all of Plato's writings; and (2) that for the most part it has not been historians of philosophy in the traditions of continental philosophy or analytic philosophy who have noted the importance of this passage for philosophy of religion. In fact, analytic historians of philosophy have eschewed this passage largely because it only indirectly

33

relates to the language issues that are their primary concern; this passage only tangentially affects their concern in the *Sophist* for monadic and relational predication.[1]

Rather, process philosophers such as Whitehead and Hartshorne, as well as Leonard Eslick and Robert Neville, have done yeoman's work to alert philosophers to this passage in Plato hitherto undervalued. At least three other critics have noticed the *potential* importance of this passage, even if they ultimately try to dissuade us from taking it too seriously. My procedure will be to treat these three thinkers first before moving to the process philosophers, all of whom claim that the idea that being *is* power is crucial. After treating Whitehead and Eslick, however, we will see that there is a significant disagreement between Neville and Hartshorne regarding *why* this claim is crucial.

VARIOUS CRITICS

A. E. Taylor doubted if the definition of being as power (*dynamis*) was ever intended seriously by Plato. Rather, Taylor thinks, Plato uses this definition merely to get a concession from the materialists that the forms have real being. That is, if the materialists (the "giants") themselves use the notion of power or force as the criterion of reality, then they have already surrendered their materialism in that forms have *dynamis*.[2]

Likewise, a more recent interpreter, J. N. Findlay, has seen the passage as dangerous because it can "readily be misinterpreted." The point to the passage, according to Findlay, is to reiterate the Platonic commonplace that the bodiless *eide* effect genuine change in souls and through souls in bodies. *Eide* make a difference. A philosopher as refined as Plato, Findlay thinks, would be unlikely to identify being with "so derivative and complex a notion as the Power to do or suffer."[3]

An initial difficulty with the Taylor-Findlay view can be seen when F. M. Cornford's commentary is consulted. *Dynamis* is the substantive answering to the verb *to be able* (*dynasthai*)—hence it makes sense that it is the root of our word *dynamic*—and it covers the ability to be acted upon as well as the ability to act on something else. *Dynamis* includes activity as well as passive capacity, as in a hand being able to act on a stone *and* being able to be acted upon by ice.[4] In addition to the technical significance of *dynamis* in medicine, the passive *dynamis* also refers to the sensitive power of being seen and of being sensitively (persuasively) influenced.[5] Regarding the latter, it is interesting to notice that both the eye and the object seen are, on the ancient Greek view, alike in being active and passive powers that unveil "the inmost and hidden nature of things," according to Cornford, just as the "real things" identified by the medical writers and Aristotle are essentially *dynameis*. Curiously, however, at the end of his commentary on the passage in question, Cornford supports the views of Taylor and Findlay to the effect that Plato does not *really* regard power as the definition of real being.[6]

By way of contrast to Taylor, Findlay, and to a lesser extent Cornford, Whitehead initiates in at least two of his works the tradition within process thought of taking the passage under consideration very seriously. In *Adventures of Ideas* he holds that it is in this quotation at *Sophist* 247E that "the height of his [Plato's] genius as a metaphysician" is to be found.[7] Quite a claim! According to Whitehead, when Plato says (through the Eleatic Stranger) that it is the *definition* (*horon*) of being that it exert power and be subjected to the exertion of power, he indicates that the essence of being is to be implicated in causal action on other things, causal action that constitutes natural law as immanent rather than as externally imposed. If Plato is defining being in terms of the agency in action *and* in terms of the recipient of action, then that which is not acted upon is a mere (external) fixture rather than real (immanent) being. Action *and* reaction belong to the essence of being, though the mediation of life/soul and mind are required to provide the media of activity and passivity for the forms. This notion of a medium connecting the eternity or everlastingness of the forms with the fluency of becoming takes many shapes in Plato's dialogues, and it is certainly true that there are passages in Plato that are inconsistent with the one under consideration in this chapter.

But Plato's genius here lies in his ability to provide a *tertium quid* between the external imposition of law on the world found in Abrahamic monotheism, say, and Stoic, pantheistic immanence. That is, according to Whitehead, Plato's definition of being as power in the *Sophist* supplements his efforts in the *Timaeus* to find a moderate view between these (transcendent monotheistic and pantheistic) extremes wherein there is both (1) an active and passive divine creator (who persuades the world and dialogues with it rather than delivers to it authoritarian dictation) and (2) the action and reaction of the "created" constituents of reality. There is much to be said in favor of Whitehead's view of Plato in *Adventures of Ideas* (and in favor of Hartshorne's similar view) wherein the creation of the world (or better, the creation of civilized order) is the victory of persuasion over force. This victory, which Whitehead sees as one of the greatest intellectual discoveries in the history of religion, is made possible by the effort to incorporate both a doctrine of divine imposition of order and a doctrine of divine immanence.

A second text where Whitehead treats the concept of "being as power" is in *Modes of Thought*.[8] Here he emphasizes that "power" is the basis of our notion of "substance" (rather than the other way around) and that in both Plato and Locke one finds a prominent place for power in metaphysics, but that neither of these thinkers *fully* developed the concepts of being *as* power and of "power *as* the drive of the universe". Whitehead himself tries to develop these concepts fully, even though his Platonism is usually associated with eternal objects, an association wherein we abstract from our experience brute particularity here and now; what remains is a residue that *seems* to have no essential reference to the passage of events. That is, Whitehead's appreciation for the concept of being as power led him away from the view of the universe as static, or better, away from the view that all transition was ultimately due to "transition" among individually static forms. Forms (along with propositions), for Whitehead, are explicitly referent to process, even if they are only so implicitly, as we will see, in some of Plato's dialogues. Life/soul and motion, however, do play crucial roles in Plato's later metaphysics.[9]

The key problem in Whitehead concerns how we should conceive of what the Eleatic Stranger calls a "complete fact" (*pantelos onti—Sophist* 248E), which Whitehead thinks has seven main factors: the forms, physical elements, psyche, eros, harmony, mathematical relations, and the receptacle. In fact, Whitehead thinks that all philosophy is an endeavor to obtain a coherent system out of these diverse factors. It must be admitted that Plato's thought in his middle dialogues, in which static forms dominate, at times intrudes into his later dialogues.[10] But in the later dialogues, and especially in the *Sophist*, there is a greater sense of the complexity of the world, in that being comes to be seen not as static but as individually creative (self-moved, as in the *Phaedrus* and *Laws* X), when besouled, and as effective in the aesthetic synthesis of others in any event.[11]

Before moving to some of Whitehead's interpreters, I want to briefly amplify the above points by appeal to *Process and Reality*. Whitehead is clear regarding his "principle of relativity" (or again, his "reformed subjectivist principle") that it belongs to the nature of a being that it is potential for every becoming. In fact, in the "principle of process" itself Whitehead claims that the being of any actual entity is *constituted by* its becoming and its modifying agency; this is his way of putting Plato's point that being is power. The stubborn facts of this world have power in Whitehead, as they do in Plato and Locke; specifically, the power to have the constitutions of other particulars conditioned and the power to be conditioned by these other particulars. This power, as we will see, has profound implications for the concept of God.

Perhaps the most penetrating look at the Platonic passage in question from a Whiteheadian point of view comes in some neglected studies by the late Leonard Eslick. He noticed the following:

> The definition of being as power (*dynamis*) in the *Sophist* is often considered as an anomaly not to be explained in Plato's thought. Or else it is simply passed by in silence by commentators rapt in the vision of immobile absolute forms, and unable to see any Plato except the mythical Plato of histories of philosophy. But it is *not* an anomaly or a passing fancy. It is simply an extension of the principles of the dialectical revolution which the *Parmenides* celebrates.[12]

The revolution in the *Parmenides* to which Eslick refers centers around a consideration of the eight hypotheses in that dialogue. It is often noted that two very different kinds of unity are investigated in these hypotheses: the one-in-itself (*to hen haplos*)—which is the subject of the second, third, fifth, and seventh hypotheses. It becomes apparent, according to Eslick, that the one-in-itself is an impossibility: a form or anything else that is a one-in-itself, a simply one *and nothing else*, cannot mingle and cannot even exist or participate in being, for this would make it not simply one but two. Further (and this is the point that may be of interest to analytic philosophers who are Plato scholars), nothing can be predicated of sheer unity, in that it would then be a one among other ones that can have anything predicated of them; that is, it would then be a multiplicity.

The paradox regarding the one-in-itself of the *Parmenides*, according to Eslick, is that the famous Platonic *chorismos* or separation of the forms seems to be both necessary to, and fatal to, discourse and understanding in metaphysics. The resolution of this paradox is the work of the *Sophist*, on Eslick's view. The criticisms leveled against the one-in-itself are catastrophic for Eleatic metaphysics, but they are also catastrophic for what Aristotle calls Plato's "original" theory of (or hypothesis concerning) forms, a theory (or hypothesis) in need of revision in the later dialogues. The forms found in the *Republic*, say, are later viewed as surds, just like the letters in Socrates' dream in the *Theaetetus*, of which nothing can be significantly affirmed or denied. Or, as is indicated in the *Philebus* (63B), "For any class to be alone, solitary, and unalloyed is not altogether possible."

But if we take a one-as-being (as power), then a one can have relations (indeed it must have relations!) because it is not an absolute unity but rather a unity somehow connected to other unities. It is a one and a one among many, a same in relation to others; it is simultaneously being and (relative) nonbeing or otherness. These consequences follow for Plato, as Eslick sees things, not by eristic manipulation and equivocation but by real necessity. Plato admits the existence of both corporeal and incorporeal things, of both subjects and predicates. On Eslick's interpretation, being as power is claimed to be that which is inherent in both of these pairs.

Knowing and being known are *each* active and passive conditions, in Eslick's view. Being as known, insofar as it is known, is moved since it is acted upon. For a form to be known by mind, it must be seen in a context of changing relationships that are other than itself. It is no longer completely at rest but partially "moved" relative to other forms and other real things. In other words, if there is no motion, if the forms do not mingle, there is no mind. However, if *all* things are in flux, mind is also destroyed. In the language of the *Cratylus* (440), to believe in universal flux is "to believe that all things leak like a pot, or imagine that the world is a man who has a running at the nose." If reality were absolute change, knowledge would be impossible because every term would resolve into its relations. Being is therefore between the Scylla and Charybdis of universal rest and universal motion, between Parmenides and Heraclitus (the two hiding places for the sophist). Like a crying child, one must plead for both the immovable and the movable (*Sophist* 249C–D). Being is a third, in addition to motion and rest.

Our discourse, when seen as a power, is derived from the interweaving of forms.[13] But this does not mean that Plato has completely abandoned the doctrine of *chorismos*. Being participates in *both* the form "in relation" and the form "in itself." As Plato puts the point in the *Seventh Letter* (343B–C), "there are two separate things, the real essence and the quality, and the soul seeks to know not the quality but the essence." He goes on to say, as Eslick notices, that knowledge is defective *in the sense that* we can never get to the essence, to the one-in-itself, only to the (relative) nonbeing that the essence has in a context of relations with others. As Eslick puts the point: "Predicates in Platonic dialectic are always and only masks worn by subjects which never appear in discourse.... Platonic dialectic is the theatre in which all actors, like those in Greek tragedy, wear masks."[14]

If being is conceived in a univocal, Parmenidean way, such that it cannot admit of intrinsic difference, then all being is one. By way of contrast, Plato's view by the time of the *Sophist* seems to have been that being is dyadic: it is *both* indivisible, static unity and a divisible, dynamic whole of parts; it is *both* in itself and in relation. Because no being (not even a divine one) can be wholly self-enclosed and separated in complete isolation, it must have some power to affect or be affected by others. Every form is, in a way, one-in-itself, yet although each is *a* one, none is *the* one in that each one is reflected in the Platonic material principle of relative nonbeing or otherness. As Eslick puts the point, "The Spinozist maxim that all determination is negation is a supreme principle of Platonic dialectic."[15]

Plato is far and away Whitehead's favorite philosopher, and he believed his own metaphysics to be a systematic modern development of Plato's general point of view.[16] It is in the passage under consideration in this chapter, however, that we can appreciate why it is good Platonism to believe, as Whitehead did, that there is nothing in the real world that is merely an inert fact, that there is an interpenetration of "being" and "becoming" to the point where it even makes sense to suggest that it is the latter that is the central notion, such that the former must be defined in terms of it. Process Platonism in general seeks the forms in the facts of becoming. But Eslick's interpretation of the passage in question also emphasizes a strong analogy between each being's one-in-itself in Plato and the *ding-an-sich* in Kant (an interpretation that was also popular among romantic thinkers such as Coleridge). Both Plato and Kant wanted to save the knowledge they held to be certain by appeal to, *but only by a critical appeal to*, the one-in-itself or the *ding-an-sich* (to the extent that there is an analogy between these two). As before, being has both an in-itself and an in-relation character.

Concentrating on that aspect of being that is its in-itself character makes it possible, as Neville argues, to avoid a superficial approach to being while also avoiding Heidegger's or Derrida's critiques of the metaphysics of presence, where some logical principle is (supposedly) used to read the nature of being off of the surface of a thing. The Heideggerian critique, which also has a Kantian flavor, is alleged to extend to almost all metaphysicians from Plato to Husserl, in that all of these thinkers, it is claimed, have a common commitment to being as presence, to some logocentric superficiality or other: what does not bear a significant relation to the logical principle arbitrarily set up as the foundational standard of being is distorted or neglected. That is, according to the Heideggerian critique, Western metaphysics has created a bothersome, hierarchical, good-bad mindset.

Neville's initial response to this critique has to do with its lack of self-reflectiveness. This very critique sets up a principle—the metaphysics of presence or logocentrism—to understand the entire tradition, and hence it distorts or neglects (at least parts of) thinkers (such as Plato) for whom this principle does not apply. Neville concludes on the evidence of this inconsistency, not that Western metaphysics has been transcended or deconstructed, but that a new look at the tradition is needed. As Josiah Royce puts it: "Whenever I have most carefully revised my moral (or philosophical) standards, I am always able to see ... that at best I have been finding out, in some new light, the true meaning that was latent in old traditions.... Revision does not mean mere destruction."[17] There are many elements in Plato's philosophy that, when separated from the notion that being is power, could support a metaphysics of presence. Process philosophy's rethinking of Plato emphasizes that the Platonic theory of (or hypothesis concerning) forms developed in dialectical relation to the world of becoming. The being of forms is "prior" with respect to motion and power. As a result, the forms are definite only if they have some plurality to measure. In effect, if a one-in-itself is not a determinate object, it cannot be defined in terms of presence. And Plato's definition of being was not in terms of presence but of power.

Neville's explication of the claim that being is power in *Recovery of the Measure* centers on the notion that the being of a thing depends on its being conditioned by and conditioning other things. Things exist by virtue of being constitutively related to other things, which is "precisely the opposite of a metaphysics of presence!"[18] The relative nonbeing or otherness that characterizes being in the *Sophist* means, as we have previously seen Eslick emphasize, that absence is just as much constitutive of being as presence. A one-in-itself is not a determinate thing; hence it cannot be defined in terms of presence. And a one-in-relation is characterized by relative nonbeing or otherness; hence it has as much to do with absence as presence. Either way, there are severe difficulties for those critics of presence who are also critics of Plato, who have not taken seriously Plato's claim (through the Eleatic Stranger) that being *is* power.

There is agreement on the part of Neville that there is something defective about a metaphysics of presence, but he denies that a properly conceived metaphysics based on the concept that "being is dynamic power" is a metaphysics of presence. This denigration of a metaphysics of presence, however, is consistent with Neville's philosophy of time, a philosophy that contains a belief that is a commonplace in process thought: the present moment contains the creative power that actualizes possibilities.[19] When the being in question is a human being, then this creative power in the present moment can be enormous, especially in saintly beings who have noteworthy power over themselves and who are in possession of the desire that is the most powerful of all, love.[20] These admissions on the part of Neville will be crucial in the following section, where he will be contrasted to Hartshorne.

A CRITIQUE OF OMNIPOTENCE

If the term *metaphysics* refers, as Hartshorne thinks it does, to the noncontingent features of reality, such that any experience confirms these features, but none falsifies them, then "being is power" is a metaphysical claim. Its scope is as wide as reality itself, from the least significant creature to God. But if it is true that being is power, then it is not only the concept of "being" that is Platonic, but also the concept of God. Two works of Hartshorne can be used to illustrate his view regarding the relationship between being and God: his early work, *Man's Vision of God*, and the more recently published volume in the Library of Living Philosophers Series, *The Philosophy of Charles Hartshorne.*[21]

In their ultimate individuality, beings, if they are instances of dynamic power, can be influenced by God, but they cannot be utterly coerced. As Hartshorne puts the point, "power is influence, perfect power is perfect influence." Or again, to have perfect power over all individuals is not to have all power. The greatest possible power (i.e., perfect power) over individuals cannot leave them powerless if being *is* power. Hence even perfect power must leave something for others to decide. In a way, even passivity is a type of activity; it is that sort of activity that takes account of, and renders itself appropriate to, the activities of others. Hence we can understand why Hartshorne claims that

> power must be exercised upon something, at least if by power we mean influence, control; but the something controlled cannot be absolutely inert, since the merely passive, that which has no active tendency of its own, is nothing; yet if the something acted upon is itself partly active, then there must be some resistance, however slight, to the "absolute" power, and how can power which is resisted be absolute?[22]

If being is power, then any relation in which one of the related things was wholly powerless would be a relation in which "the thing" was absolutely nothing: an impossibility. No matter how lowly a thing may be, if it is a real individual it reacts upon things; cells, molecules, and electrons do not provide exceptions to the view of being as power.[23]

Hartshorne agrees that God has universal relevance, and this is largely due to divine omnibenevolence. Hence there is nothing completely uninfluenced or completely outside of divine influence or love. But this Platonic view of a God who benevolently creates *ex hyle* (from beings already in existence) is a far cry from the view of God who omnipotently creates things *ex nihilo*. We can utter the words "God is omnipotent" or "God has all power," but we cannot really conceive what these words mean if there are other beings in existence, as Hartshorne eloquently argues:

> That God cannot "make us do" certain things does not "limit" his power, for there is no such thing as power to make nonsense true, and "power over us" would not be power over *us* if our natures and actions counted for nothing. No conceivable being could do more with us than God can ... and so by definition his power is perfect, unsurpassable. But it is a power unique in its ability to adjust to others.[24]

The purpose of the present chapter is not to establish that if it is true that being is power then panpsychism is true, but I would at least like to show that it is plausible to suggest that Plato held a version of panpsychism similar to that held by certain process thinkers. Metaphysical explanation, it seems, must be in terms of (a) soul—including forms as thought by besouled beings; (b) matter; or (c) both soul and matter. Materialism (b) obviously was anathema in Plato's dialogues, but it is not necessarily the case that Plato was a dualist (c). It should be remembered that in Plato's dialogues we learn that soul is the universal cause (*aitias tou holou*—*Epinomis* 988D), that it is metaphysically prior to body (*presbyteras e somatos*—*Laws* 892A), that bodies are derived from soul (*soma de deuteron te kai hysteron*—*Laws* 896C), that we receive our being from soul (*Laws* 959A), and that soul is the primary source of all things (*psychen genesis hapanton einai proten*—*Laws* 899C). Although Plato was obviously not in a position to understand a more recent panpsychism based on contemporary physics and cell theory, it would be a mistake to assume that his only options, once materialism was refuted, were to return to primitive animism or to defend dualism.[25] The possibility that Plato was a metaphysical panpsychist (a) is supported by his presumed belief in the *Sophist* that being is the power to affect or be affected by others. I take it that this "or" (*eite*) does not refer to mutual exclusivity between influence and being influenced. Once again, *omni*potent power would be an unintelligible power over the powerless and the un-influence-able.[26]

Hartshorne follows Whitehead in criticizing divine omnipotence because it conflicts with the concept of being as power.[27] Neville, however, sees beneath the dyadic character of being (in-itself and in-relation), beneath being as power, to a different "ghostly dyad": somethingness as opposed to absolute nothingness. Real things are brought into existence by an omnipotent God who creates *ex nihilo*. Or at least, for Neville, God's will is omnipotent in the long run. (The qualification is needed to deal, however inadequately, with the notorious theodicy problem that occurs if God is omnipotent.) It follows from Neville's line of reasoning that the dynamic power of particular beings is illusory, in that, if God really is omnipotent, then every apparent exercise of finite power is really an exercise of God's power. Neville actually seems to welcome this (problematic) conclusion: "Creation *ex nihilo* is the most thorough and absolute expression of power, requiring neither objects to exert power on nor a medium through which to express it."[28] Repeatedly, however, Neville does talk about the finite power of creatures, a finite power that is, on his line of reasoning, either illusory or a concession to popular religious speech.[29]

Equally problematic as Neville's view is that of Seth Bernadete in his commentary on the *Sophist*. Bernadete thinks that, as a consequence of the definition of being as power, we can conclude that the highest being would be one that affected everything else but was never itself affected.[30] This view is implausible due to the logic of dipolar theism, as we will see later. Bernadete's view is nonetheless compatible with the traditional (Nevillean, not Platonic) theology regarding divine omnipotence and creation *ex nihilo*.

A treatment of Paul Weiss' concept of "*dynamis*" would require another whole chapter. He oddly shows similarities to both Hartshorne and Neville, but his view seems to be closer to the latter than to the former. For example, in *Reality* he claims that, because it is not yet, the future cannot exert power like the present; yet he also claims that God is omnipotent. And in *The God We Seek* he talks of the sheer power of God and of God's omnipotence. Finally, to conclude this cursory glance at Weiss, consider his *Modes of Being*. Here he admits that each mode of being exerts a characteristic power and that each actuality has its own dynamic power. He nonetheless also claims that God's power is unlimited and that God is omnipotent. Weiss is quite clear that there is a conflict between divine omnipotence and the powerful modes of being other than God, but he does not resolve the conflict. Somehow or other, the modes of being merge with God.[31]

I stated earlier that it has not been historians of philosophy in the traditions of analytic or continental philosophy who have paid sufficient attention to the claim that being is power, but process philosophers. Despite the difficulties with Neville's defense of both divine omnipotence and the claim that being is power, he is certainly on the mark regarding why continental philosophy's critiques of a metaphysics of presence do not apply to Plato's definition of being in the *Sophist*. I will return to Heidegger later in the chapter. Here I would like to add some comments regarding why analytic philosophers might have a difficult time appreciating the importance of this definition.[32]

The beginning of the *Sophist* finds the characters Socrates and Theodorus agreeing that there is something significant in philosophical discourse; it need not be mere verbal dispute (216B). But because the character Socrates fades out of the picture early on, and because the philosopher is distinguished from the statesman (217A), it is clear that the view of the philosopher and the forms as defended by the character Socrates in the *Republic*, say, is not that examined in the *Sophist*. Plato's views here are presumably expressed by the Eleatic Stranger, who is on the hunt for the sophist in order to show *how* significant philosophical discourse really is possible; he is on the hunt for *real* being (*ta onta hos*) and not merely for what can be predicated of the word *being*.

In that the Stranger prefers dialectical exchanges to long speeches (217C–E), it is clear that he is not distinguished from the sophist in being a trader in words, but the *way* he trades in words does distinguish him. The sophist fosters a stupidity (*amathia*—229C) that can be exposed by a philosopher in dialectical cross-examination (230B–C). In this cross-examination, the philosopher uses persuasive devices that make him resemble a sophist as a dog does a wolf. The difference between the two lies in the fact that the sophist is unable or unwilling to create a proper likeness (*eikon*) of real being, but only constructs an inadequate semblance (*phantasma*—236B). The sophist has a fetish for discourse at the expense of the effort to mirror the truth (240A).

It must be admitted that it is not only the sophist who bothers Plato; the Stranger seems to indicate to us that Plato is also irked by those who talk about the way things really are (*hos estin*—243B) without specifying what they mean by reality. Hence there is some reason to be supportive of a linguistic turn in the doing of the history of philosophy on the basis of the *Sophist*. The naive foundationalism that the Stranger opposes is exhibited in the battle between the giants and the gods (246A–49D). The former are the materialists, and the latter defend their position—the earlier version of the forms in Plato's middle dialogues—somewhere in the heights of the unseen. It is crucial to notice that, in response to this debate, Plato does not retreat from metaphysics (nor should contemporary Platonists move unquestioningly into the arms of those who defend the linguistic turn), but rather he tries to develop an improved theory regarding real being, a theory wherein being is seen as dynamic power (247E). The battle (*mache*) between the giants and gods does indeed cause ennui, but metaphysics in general is not the least bit boring to Plato. One can, in fact, talk good sense about reality (249C–E, 250E).

It makes sense, for example, to say both that we ought not to admit that there are arbitrary breaks in nature and that our own ability to experience is part of nature. If both of these claims are correct, then it follows that throughout reality there is dynamic power, that reality is best described in panpsychist or panexperientialist terms, to use David Ray Griffin's designation. And if panexperientialism is correct, there is good reason to be suspicious of both divine omnipotence, in the sense of a monopoly of power over the powerless, and its attendant doctrine of creation *ex nihilo*.

Jon Levenson shows that the doctrine of creation out of chaos (i.e., creation *ex hyle*) is reflected not only in the first chapter of Genesis but also throughout the Hebrew Bible in that this doctrine was central to the cultic life of the Hebrew people. Christian scholars, too, have long accepted the fact that creation *ex nihilo* is not to be found in Genesis. This view does not emerge until the intertestamental literature, particularly 2 Maccabees. Gerhard May, for example, shows that the doctrine of creation *ex nihilo* was not defended by Christian thinkers until the end of the second century as a response to Marcion's gnosticism. Up until that time Christian thinkers considered the biblical view of creation to be quite compatible with the creation out of chaos found in Plato's *Timaeus*. In effect, just as Plato's apparent belief in God as the World Soul is similar to the view found in some biblical passages and finds echoes in Origen and St. Paul and in the traditional divine attribute of omnipresence, so also Plato's apparent belief that being is dynamic power (a belief that is at odds with the claim that God is omnipotent in the sense of having a monopoly of power over the powerless and who creates the world *ex nihilo*) is compatible with the biblical view of creation *ex hyle*. For all we can tell, creativity or Platonic self-motion (whether divine or nondivine) is itself uncreated.[33]

On Hartshorne's view, this critique of divine omnipotence does not demean God. The key is to hold that God's power is not separate from divine beauty and goodness; indeed, divine beauty and goodness are the divine power to inspire worship. Moreover, divine agency in the world is persuasive, rather than coercive, as evidenced in the *Timaeus*. The supposed recalcitrance of the material, on this view, is actually the problem of harmonizing the self-motions of an infinite number of partially free centers of dynamic power. God's actuality (i.e., how God exists), if not God's existence, is conditioned by states of affairs of which God is not the sole cause. Whitehead sees (Platonic) divine persuasion especially revealed in Jesus.[34]

Classical theists such as Norman Geisler will no doubt object to the efforts to, in effect, Judaize or Christianize Plato's view of God. Divine supremacy, it will be alleged, requires that God be sovereign over everything in the world, including evil. Of course this logically leads to the perennial question concerning why God does not eliminate the evil. We have seen, however, that Plato's definition of being in the *Sophist* (247D–E), the most sophisticated definition he offers, is that being is power (*dynamis*—which, once again, is not accidentally the root of our word *dynamic*), specifically the power to affect *or* to be affected by others. We have also seen that this "or" (*eite*) does not refer to mutual exclusivity between influence and being influenced. Plato's dialogue style indicates this. One does something with (not to) one's dialectical partner. This makes the dialectical style a good model for the general nature of reality. As opposed to the authoritarian dictation that Geisler and other classical theists desire from God, in dialectic it "will not do to reason as though to speak and be heard are noble, while to listen and hear are not."[35] This is made explicit in at least one dialogue, the *Gorgias* (508A). Further, to speak of the supreme soul, the World Soul, as persuading other souls is to suggest that each lesser soul has the power to be moved and that the World Soul is capable of receiving influence.

The lack of complete order in the world is at least partly explained by there being many self-movers. These many self-active agents imply indefinitely great, if not complete, disorder unless there is a "supreme soul to 'persuade' the many lesser souls to conform to a cosmic plan. They cannot completely fit such a plan for then they would not be self-determined."[36] That is, process theodicy is essentially Platonic because the divine plan cannot be completely definite and detailed. The meaning of "God has power over us" only makes sense on a Platonic view if God is a self-moved mover of others who is partially moved by these other self-movers. God can "rule the world" by setting optimal limits for free action. The divine can control the changes in us by inspiring us with novel ideas; by molding the divine life God presents at each moment a partly new ideal. *Omni*potent power would therefore be a monopoly of power over the powerless; but Hartshorne agrees with the Platonic claim that being *is* power, hence "to be an individual is to decide."[37] Decision means the cutting off of some possibilities rather than others (literally: de-cision), a cutting off that is not necessarily done self-consciously.

DYNAMIC STRUGGLE

Throughout Plato's dialogues there is the assumption that without philosophy we are like somewhat helpless prisoners largely compelled to view the world in ignorance (*Phaedo* 82E). We would remain in this helpless state if there were not some sort of existence for nonexistence. If nonbeing had no being whatsoever, then we would be very much controlled by the fear found in the *Euthydemus* (286D–87A), *Cratylus* (429D), and *Theaetetus* (188D, 189B) that it would be impossible to tell a lie, in that a lie consists in deliberately saying that what is not the case is the case, or vice versa. But it is obvious that there are liars. So also it would be impossible to think falsely in that such thinking consists in believing what is not the case is the case, or vice versa. But it is obvious that we can make mistakes. Luckily we can avoid these undesirable results due to the fact that in the later dialogue the *Sophist* (237–41) there is a distinction drawn between absolute nonexistence (which remains impossible) and relative nonexistence or otherness, which is claimed to exist as a result of the parricide on "father Parmenides" (who denied the existence of any sort of nonexistence).

It makes sense to say that at times we make mistakes (or lie) when we mistakenly (or deliberately) say that something is the case when it is not the case (when something other than what is the case is claimed to be the case).[38] Even the forms are affected by this discovery in that, although each form is something, there may be things that each of them is not. This "is not" does not refer to something contrary to what exists, but rather to something within the realm of existence that is different or other from something else that exists (*Sophist* 256D–58B).

Although Heidegger correctly notices the discovery of relative nonbeing in the *Sophist*, he does not adequately explicate the importance of this discovery in its relation to the definition of being as *dynamis*. Indeed, Heidegger trivializes the importance of this definition. He does so in two ways. First, as a result of the poetic license Heidegger grants himself to translate Greek terms rather loosely for his own purposes, he sees the definition of being as power as one that "later will show itself as something else." He moves from Plato "offering" a definition to "proffering" one and from there to "pre-offering" one, all on the slim evidence of *proteinomenon*: a cognate of the infinitive "to put forward" or "to offer." Second, although Heidegger notices that Hermann Bonitz translates *dynamis* as "dynamic" or "living power," he prefers to translate it as "possibility." In fact, he thinks that "dynamic power" cannot even be taken seriously as a translation of *dynamis* in this passage. What sense would it make, he seems to be asking, to define being as dynamic or living power? A great deal of sense, I have been arguing in this and the previous chapter, given the evidence in favor of panpsychism in the *Laws*, the absence of any notion of divine omnipotence or creation *ex nihilo* in Plato's dialogues, and the resolution of the battle of the "giants" and the "gods" in the *Sophist* (a resolution that suggests that both sides in this dispute have alerted us to types of being or dynamic power operative in the cosmos).[39]

If we take seriously the definition of being as power, as presented by the Eleatic Stranger in the *Sophist*, then we can understand why reality is as hard to understand as unreality. The battle between the "giants" (materialists who drag everything down to earth and who affirm as real only that which can be seen or that which can resist touch) and the "gods" (the friends of forms who claim that the real is to be found somewhere in the heights of the unseen) can be resolved on the basis of this definition in that *anything* has real being if it can affect or be affected by any others. Both material and formal beings are real, on the basis of this definition, as are things that change as well as things that do not change (*Sophist* 245D–48C). Of course throughout Plato's dialogues various *dynameis* have been posited, dynamic powers that are, on the basis of the definition in the *Sophist*, given real being: love (*Symposium* 205D), knowledge (*Republic* 518C, 534C), and many other things that are capable of action and/or passion in their interaction with each other by way of similarities and differences (*Theaetetus* 156A, 157A, 159A, 159D, 182B). Thus, being is parceled out, as it were, from greatest to smallest (*Parmenides* 144B).

The divine reality is distinctive not in terms of creativity as such, but rather in terms of the extent and quality of its creativity, of the ability to act in a qualitatively superior way on/with a greater number of beings than the rest of us. God's creative effort to bring order out of what would otherwise be disorderly chaos is fair (*kalon*—*Timaeus* 27C–29D, 68E). Indeed, the cosmos is as perfect as possible, according to the character Socrates in the *Timaeus* (39D–41D). Our ability to think makes us especially like the divine among created things in that we can be reflective cocreators of an orderly life (*Timaeus* 44D). Without rational planning, whatever harmony that exists, either in our own lives or in the cosmos in general, would be purely accidental (*Timaeus* 44D, 69B–C; also see 74D, 75D, 76C, 91A). Although our ability to create an orderly pattern only results in a semblance (*phantasma*) of the ideal, whereas God can create a true likeness (*eikon*) of the ideal, it is clear that human beings nonetheless are like God in having at least some creative power allied to reason, as the Eleatic Stranger (presumably Plato) sees things in the *Sophist* (236B, 265B–68D).

Ancient chaos reasserts itself whenever the divine principle of limit is abandoned or forgotten or rejected; at these times our lives hover on the brink of destruction. In any event, the cosmos at any particular time is a mixture of limit and unlimit, a besouled whole that orders in as good a way as possible its diverse self-movers (see *Statesman* 273B–C; *Philebus* 27B–C, 28D–30D). Plato wavers, however, especially through the Athenian in the *Laws*, between seeing divine purpose in the overall orderliness and harmony of the cosmos and seeing it in the details, in particular places and natural events. But at no point is there evidence that God controls everything that happens, a view that would be at odds with the definition of being as dynamic power (see *Laws* 740A, 741C, 752D, 775C–E, 782B, 873E; *Epinomis* 979A, 983E–84C, 985D, 991B).

Of course Plato does not go out of his way to have one of the characters in his dialogues state explicitly an opposition to divine omnipotence, conceived as a monopoly of power, as does Hartshorne in his book *Omnipotence and Other Theological Mistakes*. The reason is simple: no one before Plato had asserted such a doctrine; hence there was no need to refute it. However, such an opposition is often implied in Plato's dialogues, an opposition that surfaces in the oddest places, as when Agathon in the *Symposium* argues that even love (Aphrodite), the mightiest of all, must contend with necessity (196D–97B). And in the *Republic* it is clear that any rational agent is confronted eventually with the spindle of necessity and the fates (Lachesis, Clotho, and Atropos), which are mythically portrayed as the daughters of necessity (616C, 617C, 619C, 620E–21B; also see *Laws* 960C–D). In the strongest statement to this effect, we find the character Socrates in the *Theaetetus* stating that it is necessity that binds together our existence. Theaetetus even compares Socrates to necessity: neither can be avoided (160B, 169C; also see *Parmenides* 149A).

In the creation myth of the *Timaeus*, however, can be found the most extensive Platonic treatment of the necessity (*anangke*) that resists any besouled agency, whether divine, human, or subhuman. God wants everything to be good and nothing to be bad so far as this is attainable (*bouletheis gar ho theos agatha men panta, phlauron de meden einai kata dynamin*— 30A). The point is reiterated several times (46D, 48A, 53B, 56C, 68E). This resistance to divine goodness seems to be one of the "laws of destiny" (*nomous te tous heimarmenous*—41E).

I assume that there is a family resemblance among several words for conditions that are beyond the ability of any good self-mover, even God, to control: necessity (*anangke*), fate (*moira*), chance (*tyche*), or destiny (*heimarmene*). In the *Laws* it becomes apparent that the human lawgiver is confounded with the same sort of problems that God confronts in the creation of an orderly world: resistant chance and infinitely variable circumstance (i.e., an infinite number of self-movers) get in the way. Self-mover A is responsible for moving to spot X at time Y; and self-mover B is responsible for moving to spot X at time Y; but no one is responsible for A and B accidentally crashing at spot X at time Y. The crash is "due to" chance or fate. Like a skilled navigator, one must negotiate one's way through the tempest. Or better, along with God we do not so much contend *against* necessity (which would apparently be futile) as work with it or cajole it so as to elicit as much order and limit and goodness as is needed so as to bring about a beautiful world: in ourselves, in our political institutions, and in the natural world (see *Laws* 709A–C, 710D, 741A, 818B–E, 901D; also see *Epinomis* 982C; and *Third Letter* 316D).[40]

There is always over and above law (whether divine law in the cosmos or human law in science or politics) a factor of the "simply given" or "brute fact." It is this surd or irrational element that Plato refers to as necessity in the *Timaeus*. When the evidence of this dialogue is considered in conjunction with that of the definition of being as dynamic power in the *Sophist*, one is tempted to think in a Hartshornian way that Plato was working his way toward, or at least he could have easily worked his way toward, the view that this surd is nothing other than the stubborn fact of the clash of a multitude of self-movers.

Chapter Three

Forms As Items in
Divine Psychical Process

Introduction

The Platonic view of God that I am defending in the present book is now starting to take shape. God's omnipresence as the soul for the body of the world and God's preeminent and ideal (yet not omnipotent) power are crucial parts of this view. But no view of God that is Platonic can afford to ignore the question regarding the relationship between God and the forms. It is the purpose of the present chapter to articulate this relationship.

At least two classic alternatives are open to consideration. These alternatives have been carefully examined by Harry Wolfson, which he labeled as the "extradeical" and the "intradeical" interpretations of the subject matter in question.[1] On the former interpretation, the forms are separate from both the material world *and* the divine mind, thus possessing a mysterious independent existence on their own. On the latter interpretation to be defended in the present chapter, however, the forms are items in divine, and to a lesser extent human, psychical process. I will rely on Hartshorne more than Whitehead in this defense (without thereby implying that Hartshorne and Whitehead are as far apart as some suppose regarding their views of universals and eternal objects, respectively).[2]

Later in the chapter I will show the implications of this view for claims regarding both divine omniscience and omnibenevolence.

Forms as Items in Divine Psychical Process

What does it mean to explain the world philosophically? At the very least, it means to elucidate the unitary principle behind the apparent duality of

51

mind (or soul) and matter. Plato wavers, according to Hartshorne, between seeing this principle in the forms and seeing it in soul (psyche). Hartshorne emphasizes the difficulty in offering an explanation through a form that is not really an explanation through soul. The neoplatonists were justified in interpreting the forms as divine ideas, inseparable from intelligence (*nous*); and Plato gives some warrant for this interpretation when he makes the Demiurge ideally aware of the highest form, that of the good. That is, the forms are items internal to psychical process.[3]

This view obviously conflicts with what has been, until recently, the standard account that for Plato the forms are "independent" even of God (i.e., the extradeical account). Hartshorne thinks that Plato was brighter than this, even if some passages in the dialogues can be cited that seem to support this account. If "X is independent of Y" has a sharp logical meaning it must be that X could exist even if Y did not, which implies that Y is contingent. If X stands for the forms and Y for God, then the nonexistence of God is being taken as possible. But this "possibility" conflicts not only with the treatments of God in the *Timaeus* and *Laws* X, but also with Plato's flirtation with the ontological argument, to be discussed later in chapter 5. If the Demiurge is not contingent, then not only are the forms envisaged by deity, but they *could not* lack this status.

It is true for Hartshorne that things that are more abstract than events (or events collected together as an individual) may be primordial in a vicarious way if they are always found embodied in inherited events. But he only sees the *most* abstract universals—the metaphysical principles themselves—as "eternal" in this sense. They precede every event. Further, this Hartshornian doctrine is a version of the view found in Plato's dialogues that forms are known by reminiscence in that memory is an ingredient in thought as such. But it is an "unplatonic Platonism"; unplatonic, at least, on many interpretations of Plato.[4] Abstraction from the concrete proceeds backward in time and depends on memory because one may abstract from each instance but not from all—another instance will always do, but none at all will not do.[5] It is true that in Plato's middle dialogues forms "are not literal descriptions of things, but unattainable limits, *ideals* to which things may approximate in varying degrees."[6] For example, the ideal of absolute equality discussed in the *Phaedo* (74) is so unattainable that any sufficiently accurate measurement of the length, say, of two things will reveal some slight difference between two "equal" things; or at least no measurement is accurate enough to prove that there is not a difference. So also with the form of straightness, and so on.

Hartshorne's partial disagreement with Whitehead on eternal objects is largely due to Whitehead's "Platonic" fascination with this particular ("atypical") feature of mathematical universals; that is, their extreme abstractness and generality. Hartshorne does not think that Whitehead's notion of God would be hurt if one eliminated the idea of eternal species, for example, while retaining that of eternal highest genera, including the genus of specificity as such.[7] Even with regard to mathematical forms there is a sense in which these ideals are "literally actualized."[8] For example, if there are two horses and two cows in a field, then the number of horses is exactly, not approximately, equal to the number of cows. It is because concrete things can be equal to each other that the abstraction "equality" is made possible.[9] And it is Plato, at least "as he is usually interpreted," who is responsible for the error that what one knows in mathematics is pure being above becoming, devoid of life and power.[10] (A consideration of the definition of being as power in the *Sophist* changes this estimation considerably, however.) Hartshorne agrees with Stephen Korner that Plato discovered not so much ideas as ideals.[11]

As before, however, the theory of forms as items in divine psychical process gives us a different view of Plato, a view that depends on the necessary existence of deity. If one asks whether the forms have supremacy over God, Hartshorne's response would be that "the issue is secondary and largely verbal."[12] The good and God are both everlasting, and independence has no clear meaning between everlasting things. (Once again, let us assume here that "everlasting" refers to something that exists through all of time and "eternal" refers to an existence that is outside of time altogether.) Because God always contemplates the good, this contemplation is an everlasting idea (of an Idea or Form). What could be gained by asking if forms would exist if they were not divine ideas, except the (erroneous) conclusion that God is a mere fact that perhaps comes to be, perhaps not? But for Hartshorne (and Plato, he alleges) there is never an alternative to the contemplation of the good by the supreme being. Only the most extreme types of "Platonism" (i.e., the extradeical view), not necessarily held by Plato, would see abstract entities as real in themselves apart from all concrete embodiment, say in some concrete process of thinking. The basic reality is concrete even if the most fundamental abstraction is concreteness as such. Metaphysics itself is "the study of the abstraction 'concreteness.'" Hartshorne is not so bold to claim that Plato quite saw that concrete actualities are the whole of what is, but he came close enough to seeing this in his thoughts on God in the later dialogues so as to confound traditional extradeical interpretations of Plato's forms as absolutely independent of concrete embodiment.[13]

How does Hartshorne's treatment of Plato's forms in his own philosophy (he refers to them as "ideas" or "universals") differ from Whitehead's treatment of Plato's forms? Whitehead believes in many eternal realities, including the metaphysical categories, the primordial nature of God, and eternal objects. In a similar manner, for Hartshorne the metaphysical categories (and mathematical ideas) are everlasting, but only in the ways elucidated above. He rejects Whitehead's term *eternal objects* and usually returns to the traditional term *universals* in order to avoid the impression that the most abstract entities transcend creative process altogether, an impression that Whitehead would presumably like to avoid as well. Although the metaphysical categories are always instantiated, and hence are eternal (or better, everlasting), the other universals are emergent and contingent, as in "different from Shakespeare," or as in the precise shade and hue of blue in a certain iris or in a certain experience of the flower. Hartshorne cannot call these universals "eternal," as would Whitehead in his somewhat more "extreme form of Platonism." But in this rejection Hartshorne nonetheless thinks he has Plato on his side. Hartshorne is not convinced that all truths, even those concerning universals, are timeless for Plato.[14]

From Peirce Hartshorne has learned that the past is the sum of accomplished facts, but there are additions to the past that occur at every moment. These actualities (events, not things) become but they do not change, if change refers to the succession of these events. Once an actuality comes to be, it remains forever an indestructible item in the past. Thus it is false to say that all actualities change (none of them do!) and false to say that the past never really is. Plato is correct, on Hartshorne's view, that what is worth knowing is permanent, for past events and "emerged" universals have a reality that is forever. "Change is addition to, not subtraction from, reality. ... Plato's greatness is that, more than anyone else, he almost saw even the things that he failed to see." Over and over in Plato's dialogues we learn that unless we know the past of something we do not understand it.[15] This is another way of saying that the past of something is included in deity, and only in a profoundly different way is the future so included. Much of what Whitehead wants from eternal objects Hartshorne wants as well, but the desired result can more reasonably be gained from the everlasting and the theory of emergent universals. Presumably Whitehead would say that God could not know which eternal object an occasion will select, but God could know all the possibilities. Hartshorne's point is that the occasion "does not merely 'select' from fully determinate potentialities, but that it renders the determinable determinate."[16]

Of course I have presumed too much in alleging what Whitehead's relationship with Plato is; indeed it is a complex relationship, as John Cobb and others have legitimately emphasized. Lewis Ford argues that Hartshorne is not very much at odds with Whitehead regarding eternal possibilities. And Ivor Leclerc notices that Whitehead is not necessarily committed to the notion that forms are *ousiai* or separate actualities, in that he is an Aristotelian to the extent that he insists that forms are forms of *ousiai*. Nor does Whitehead believe—as does Plato, according to Leclerc—that forms are perfect archetypes that are specific in number. Nonetheless, Leclerc admits that Whitehead, along with Plato, sees that to recognize an element of form exhibited by many actualities necessitates that we acknowledge form as a distinct metaphysical category. (Even Hartshorne could admit this much.) Whitehead also believes, according to Leclerc, that form, although not separate from actualization, does have some "nature" transcending actuality. It is perhaps because of this "nature" that A. W. Levi calls Whitehead a "Platonic realist."[17]

My point has been to claim that Hartshorne's theory of emergent universals and his theory of forms as items in divine psychical process do not necessarily make his debt to Plato less than that of Whitehead. Hartshorne's distaste for eternal objects is meant as a criticism of a certain variety of "Platon*ism*," which distorts what is central in Whitehead's philosophy: creative synthesis.[18] Hartshorne does believe that Whitehead follows the Neoplatonists and Plato himself (and, indeed, Hartshorne himself) in holding that forms or eternal objects are divine ideas, "nothing simply by themselves."[19] And our physical or hybrid prehensions of God as having these ideas are our best clues as to how to acquire them for ourselves. The possible disagreement between Hartshorne and Whitehead has nothing to do with the latter relying on Plato and the former eschewing Platonic influence. Rather, the major point of difference, if there is such, seems to lie with the question as to which ideas are always in God and which are acquired (divinely or humanly) as the creative process goes on.

It is an error to assume that Plato's only alternative to being determined by the past is to be determined by an ideal, for no ideal can be applied without creative particularization. An understanding of soul as self-moved sheds light on how Plato had at least an inkling of the truth that "the creative, temporal character of experiencing yields all the light upon modality as ontological that we are going to get" in that "particular and actual are essentially one, and so are universal and potential."[20]

FORMS AS ABSTRACTIONS

A Platonic "friend of the forms," to use a phrase from the *Sophist*, would presumably be opposed to Penelope Maddy's effort to bring mathematical ontology into line with a materialist worldview. Rather, for a "friend of the forms" a more fruitful effort would be to bring a scientific worldview into line with a mathematical ontology. Of course this leads to a question regarding how to accurately characterize mathematical ontology.

According to Reuben Hersh, although some mathematicians are convinced that mathematical formalism means that mathematics is just a game with inherently meaningless symbols, most mathematicians *in practice* presuppose the traditional Platonic view that mathematical entities are in a sense outside of space and time and outside of thought. But this pragmatic stance leaves unresolved a further question: do such mathematical entities have an existence outside of human thought only or outside of divine thought as well? (Presumably there are times when no mathematician is thinking about, and no mathematical text has codified, some mathematical theorem that will someday be discovered as true.) Leibniz, for example, was a latter-day Platonist (and one of the discoverers of calculus) who saw mathematical entities as thoughts in the mind of God. Because God is generally not discussed in the contemporary academic world, mathematicians and philosophers of mathematics in effect continue to believe in an independent, immaterial abstract world without a preeminent knower to think of it, much like the grin on Lewis Carroll's Cheshire cat, a grin that remained without the cat, as Hersh notices. Contemporary process Platonism consists in the effort to acknowledge the (divine) cat behind the grin, as it were.[21]

It should also be clear that defense of a contemporary version of Platonic forms has implications not only for mathematics but also for ethics. Nietzsche's "death of God," as Heidegger realized, entails the rejection of religious *values*, as well as the rejection of God's existence. Griffin refers to this as the disenchantment of the world. The reenchantment of the world, however, does not necessarily involve a return to the supernaturalist religion of classical theism, wherein God was viewed as an omnipotent tyrant who ruled the world from above it. That is, God was not seen as the soul or mind for the natural body of the world, but rather as supernatural. Nor was being seen in terms of dynamic power but rather in terms of a contingent presence that was utterly due to an omnipotent God who created the world *ex nihilo*.[22] On the classical theistic account, there would have been no world if God had not chosen to create it.

Hartshorne characterizes his own quasi-Platonic view of universals of whatever sort (mathematical, ethical, etc.) in the following terms:

> Things more abstract than events or individuals may be primordial and everlasting by proxy in being always found embodied in inherited

events. Whitehead's eternal objects are such; in my view only the most abstract universals, the metaphysical principles themselves, are eternal [or better, everlasting] in this sense. They precede *every* event ... because every event has predecessors and any event must instance the metaphysical universals. This is a sort of version of Plato's doctrine that forms are known by reminiscence. Memory is an ingredient in thought as such. But this is an unplatonic Platonism.[23]

For the sake of clarity it should be emphasized that for *both* Hartshorne and Whitehead there is a crucial distinction between actuality and possibility and that it is because of this distinction that they criticize Plato, who apparently does not identify the forms as pure possibles. All three parties can agree with the claim that forms have real being (*dynamis*), as was claimed in the previous chapter. But process thinkers are skeptical of the view of forms as perfect actualities, as detailed in Plato's middle dialogues, including the *Republic*.

According to Whitehead's ontological principle, real being is "here" rather than "there," even the real being of the forms (or eternal objects or universals, the terminology depending on the thinker in question). Even God, when seen as the soul for the body of the world, is here. As a result, neither Hartshorne nor Whitehead sees permanence as more real than flux, as Plato apparently did in his middle dialogues. Possibilities are abstractions from the actualities that are in flux, on the process view, as least as long as one includes among the actualities in flux the divine one. Thus, it is more accurate to say that forms participate in (or better, are ingredient in) things than it is to say that things participate in forms. But in such ingredience forms do not lose their status as potentials. That is, forms are not "being" if what is meant by this term is unchanging reality in contrast to becoming, but they are "being" if what is meant by this term is the belief that alternative possibilities for future becoming have a sort of dynamic power in the world.[24]

Because possibilities are abstractions from the actualities in flux, it makes sense to say, as Victor Lowe does, that Whitehead's doctrine of eternal objects and Hartshorne's doctrine of universals are as much Aristotelian as they are Platonic, despite the fact that both Whithead and Hartshorne identify themselves as modified Platonists.[25] In Whitehead's case, at least, the reason for this is the fact that Plato (who was heavily influenced by Pythagoras, as is well known) stands nearer than Aristotle to contemporary science due to his apparent belief that number lies at the base of the real world, that no understanding of either the natural or moral/religious worlds is possible without a mind that has been disciplined by a study of mathematical abstractions.[26]

DIVINE OMNISCIENCE AND OMNIBENEVOLENCE

To say that forms (conceptual possibilities) are items in divine psychical process, indeed to say that they are known ideally by God, is to come close to the claim that God is omniscient. But divine omniscience as traditionally conceived in the Abrahamic religions runs the risk of contradicting what seems to be a nonnegotiable item in Plato's later dialogues (e.g., *Phaedrus, Timaeus, Laws*): soul is defined as self-motion, as some sort of spontaneity or freedom.

Specifically, the problem is the following: if God is omniscient in the traditional sense found in the Abrahamic religions, God already knows everything that will occur in the future with absolute assurance and in minute detail; but if God has such knowledge, it is difficult, if not impossible, to see how human beings could be self-movers, for if God has such knowledge, then human beings *must* do what God knows they will do, and hence they would not be self-movers. Even if God does not physically compel human beings, if God is omniscient in the aforementioned strong sense, they are nonetheless logically compelled to do what God knows they will do. Even if a human being decides to fool God, the omniscient mind of God would know beforehand that the human being would try to do this. (Modern scientific determinism makes sense only to the extent that scientists can approximate the knowledge traditional Abrahamic theists attributed to God.)

This traditional view of omniscience implies that all events in a person's life are *internally* related to all the others, such that implicit in an infant are all the experiences of the adult, and this is due to God's eternal foreknowledge of everything that is to happen. This view is a symmetrical one in that a human being in the present is internally related not only to past phases of itself, but to future phases of itself as well. An equally disastrous view is that of Hume and Russell that, strictly speaking, there is no besouled identity, because each event in "a person's life" is *externally* related to the others. Despite the obvious differences between these two views, they are both symmetrical. That is, a theory of pure external relations, sometimes called the "drops of experience" view, leads to a symmetrical view because the present moment of a besouled life is externally related not only to "its" future phases but also to the past phases of "its" life. The process view is an asymmetrical one, by way of contrast: someone in the present is internally related to her past phases but is only externally related to her future phases, if such there be.

On a process view one can nonetheless defend a concept of 'divine omniscience' in the sense that God, as the unsurpassable being-in-becoming, would, as a consequence, have to be the unsurpassable knower. But this does not mean that God could know logical impossibilities. Rather, God knows all that is logically possible: God knows all past actualities as already actualized; all present events in their presentness (subject, of course, to the laws of physics) as they come to pass; and future possibilities (or probabilities) as possibilities (or probabilities). That is, God knows all future possibilities (or probabilities) better than any human knower, but God does not know any future actualities because none exist: the future is always at least partially indeterminate.

To claim to know a future possibility as already actualized is not an example of perfect, divine knowledge but is rather an example of ignorance or fraudulence. Obviously, it is impossible to know the concrete details of the world as God knows them, but in general outline it seems fair to say that the greatest sort of knowledge of future possibilities (or probabilities) is to know these possibilities (or probabilities) *precisely in their indeterminacy*. It is no great accomplishment to "know" the future as one knows the past, since one would then not really be knowing the future *in its futurity*. That is, the traditional view of omniscience in the Abrahamic religions is not the only way to view the matter, as we will see momentarily when I consider some texts from Plato's dialogues, especially when it is considered that the soul's self-motion—which, I take it, is a nonnegotiable item in Plato's later dialogues—presupposes that there be a certain degree of indeterminacy with respect to the future.

I claim that God is omniscient. But no being, not even God, can know with absolute assurance and in minute detail what will *in fact* happen in the future. God must be as great as possible at any particular time, or else God would not be the greatest being-in-becoming. But new moments bring with them new possibilities for greatness, which God must realize in the best way possible if God is the greatest being-in-becoming, or better, the unsurpassable. This means that God is greater than any being who is not God but that God can always—must always!—surpass previous instances of divine greatness. It does not mean that God's earlier existence was inferior, because it was at that particular time the greatest conceivable existence, the greatest existence logically possible, and greater than any other being.

Further, divine omniscience is not unrelated to divine omnibenevolence if we take seriously Plato's famous intuition about the coextensiveness of knowledge and virtue, as George Shields insightfully observes. That is, omniscience is, in a sense, the key to other divine attributes. It may very well be the case that unsurpassable (except by divinity itself) benevolence is analytic of the idea of omniscience. Hartshorne puts the matter in the following terms:

> The reason that in us knowledge is not identical with virtue is only that we mean by knowing not necessarily the actual, concrete awareness of things, but the virtual or abstract awareness of them. Thus a man may know that his acts will have harmful consequences in the sense that, if asked, he would give the right answer to questions; but it does not follow that in the precise moment of decision he has these matters present to his mind with any concreteness and correctness. However, the divine or adequate awareness cannot in this way escape the identity of knowing and valuing. While virtual and abstract knowledge has little of the values of concrete reality, actual and concrete knowledge has all the values, and cannot fail to respond; for the ability to be aware and the ability to respond are identical.[27]

An omniscient being's sympathetic participation in others' experiences eliminates negative motivations such as hatred or envy.

Once again, divine omniscience, including a pervasive divine knowledge of conceptual possibilities or forms, is essentially referent to process. Each occasion (to use Whitehead's term) combines a number of what we call "universal characters" (what are called "*ideai*" in some of Plato's dialogues), including shape and color. These universal characters (or eternal objects or forms) are, on the interpretation I am defending, intradeical. Or perhaps better, to use the language of Eric Perl, the Demiurge as pure intellect is *noesis*, and the forms as content of the demiurgic intellect are the objects of *noesis*. This interpretation, wherein God and paradigm can be intellectually distinguished but cannot be ontologically separated, enables us to better understand how, in the *Timaeus*, the cosmos is a work of art that is an image of the idea in the divine artist's mind: since this artist *is* mind, the divine artist *is*, in a way, the paradigm. This interpretation also helps us to better understand the otherwise confusing presentation in the *Sophist* of the forms as living and thinking: they are the intellectual contents of a living and thinking divine being. Even the *Republic* is illuminated by this interpretation. The otherwise confusing effort in the *Republic* to have the good function as a cause starts to be intelligible when the good is seen as the most exalted content of the mind of the divine cause, as Eugenio Benitez argues.[28]

It will be instructive at this juncture to be explicit regarding the extent to which the points made thus far in this chapter are evidenced in Plato's dialogues themselves and the extent to which they are inferences made by process thinkers on the basis of Plato's dialogues. The evidence from Plato's dialogues in favor of the claim that (a) the forms have always existed is massive, as is the evidence from the dialogues for the claims that (b) God has always existed and that (c) God (the Demiurge) knows the forms. It is Hartshorne, however, who puts these three claims together so as to reach the inference that God could not fail to know the forms; to imagine objects of knowledge that would be outside the ken of the greatest knower is impossible. So the intradeical view defended in this chapter can be seen as Platonic even if it relies on interpretation of the subject matter in question that is not made explicit in the dialogues.

Likewise, the evidence from Plato's dialogues that (d) God is all wise and the greatest knower is massive, as is evidence for the claims that (e) God is all-good and that (f) knowledge is coextensive with virtue. It is Hartshorne, however, who puts these three claims together so as to reach the inference that belief in divine omniscience is connected to belief in divine omnibenevolence. And this inference, like the first, can be seen as Platonic even if it relies on interpretation of the subject matter in question that is not made explicit in the dialogues.

Even in the early dialogues it is clear that real wisdom is divine rather than human, as Socrates makes clear in the *Apology* (23A, 42A). In fact, in comparison with God's wisdom we appear to be like the apes (*Greater Hippias* 289B; *Second Letter* 311D). This approach endures in the middle dialogues, where wisdom and knowledge are seen to be proper to the divine and are found only vicariously in human beings. This is true both with respect to moral knowledge of, say, justice, and to knowledge that is not moral in character. As is well known, the superiority of God's knowledge rests on the fact that the forms provide the content of the divine intellect, whereas we are distracted by, or at times even require, less reliable objects of "knowledge" (*Republic* 612C, 612E; also 597B). In Socrates' well-known speech in praise of love in the *Symposium* (204A), Socrates reports on Diotima's explanation regarding why a divine being does not need to seek after truth nor to long for wisdom: a divine being *already* has these. Likewise, from the character Socrates' comments in the *Phaedrus* (247D, 248C, 249C, 266B) we learn of God's ability to know the truth *simpliciter*, a knowledge impressive enough to deserve our designating it "omniscience."

The situation does not significantly change in the later dialogues (see *Timaeus* 53D, 68D; *Laws* 691B, 692B). For example, in the *Parmenides* (134C, 134E) it is claimed (by the character Parmenides—presumably Plato, who is older and wiser than the character Socrates in this dialogue) that perfect knowledge (*akribestaten epistemen*) is an entitlement of God rather than of anyone else. Divinity knows everything that is knowable (*Laws* 901D), and God is supremely wise (*sophotaton*—*Laws* 903A). It is a commonplace in Plato's dialogues that human beings too easily have their attention deflected away from the principles that make knowledge possible. It will be remembered from the above that there are two senses of the term *omniscience*, with one including definite knowledge regarding what will happen in the future (the traditional view in the Abrahamic religions) and the other involving knowledge of future possibilities (or probabilities) *as* possibilities (or probabilities). It should be noted that in Plato's dialogues foreknowledge or prevision (*prooron*) is only rarely mentioned; and when it is mentioned it is done in a way consistent with the second (process) sense of 'omniscience,' wherein preeminent knowledge of the future involves possibilities (or probabilities) rather than definiteness, otherwise it would not be knowledge *of the future* (see, e.g., *Timaeus* 70C; *Laws* 691D). In any event, it is significant that the enormous number of passages that refer to God's preeminent knowledge hardly ever have reference to what will happen in the future.

These numerous texts that point toward divine omniscience can be supplemented by texts where divine omniscience and omnibenevolence are either linked or are discussed in close proximity. In the *Phaedo* (80D, 83E), for example, the character Socrates emphasizes that God is wise and good and pure (*katharou*). And it is not surprising to find in the *Republic* (352A–B, 361B, 368A, 379B) that God is just; the implication for human beings is that they should not wish to seem but to be just, in imitation of the divine model. The character Socrates puts the matter as follows: "But as to saying that God, who is good, becomes the cause of evil to anyone, we must contend in every way that neither should anyone assert this... nor anyone hear it" (380B).[29] It seems legitimate to say that in Plato's dialogues God is omnibenevolent because God is not deficient in either beauty or excellence (*callous he aretes*—381C). In fact, it is because of Plato's commitment to divine omnibenevolence that he finds Homer's description of the gods as scurrilous to be especially scurrilous itself (e.g., 390B, 391A, 391D). To think of divinity is not to think in terms of anthropocentric categories such as deception and rape, but rather in terms of integrity and wholeness (*holou*—486A) and all that is blameless (612E, 613B, 617E; also see *Phaedrus* 246E).[30]

If the thesis that forms are items in divine psychical process makes sense, then we can understand why in Plato's dialogues the goodness of God is reiterated so often. God could not fail to contemplate the form of the good if (a) God always exists, (b) God has ideal knowledge of the forms, (c) the form of the good always exists, and (d) God is an omnibenevolent being who does not deviate from what is morally admirable. The language in the *Republic*, wherein the form of the good makes it possible that the world be intelligible to us (indeed it causes such intelligibility), can easily be accommodated by the interpretation I am offering: the form of the good should be seen here not as a divine causal agent but rather as the crucial intellectual content contemplated by a divine causal agent. Obviously other interpretations of the subject matter in question are possible, but the passages in Plato's dialogues that deal with the form of the good (e.g., *Republic* 508A–C, 508E, 532C, 540A; *Laws* 897D, 898E) do not militate against the claims that forms are items in divine psychical process and that God is omniscient/omnibenevolent.

The strong support for divine omnibenevolence found in Plato's middle dialogues continues in the late ones. It is agreed among the participants in the *Timaeus* that "God desired that all things should be good and nothing bad, so far as this was attainable" (*bouletheis gar ho theos agatha men panta, phlauron de meden einai kata dynamin*—30A). The greatest gift from God to human beings, a gift that is nothing less than providential, is philosophy itself. In fact, God is our savior (*sotera*) through the gift of intellect. There is an obvious danger at this point that terms such as *providence, savior,* and *forgiveness* (see *Philebus* 65D) would lead us into unwarranted associations with Christian understandings of these terms, but there is an equal danger involved in ignoring altogether the providential and soteriological dimensions of Plato's thoughts on God (*Timaeus* 44C, 47A–B, 48D–E). In short, evidence from the *Timaeus* seems to indicate that God tries to bring about as much good as possible, given the limits of recalcitrant necessity and multiple self-movers (see 68E, 71D).

Evidence from the comments of the Athenian (presumably Plato) in the *Laws* is consistent with the above. Human goodness, such as it is, is dependent on divine goodness, whose hallmark is not only wisdom but also pity (*eleountas*), once again pointing out the dangers of both an unquestioned assimilation of Plato's views to those in the Abrahamic religions and a refusal to compare Plato's view of God with that in the Abrahamic religions (*Laws* 631B, 642C–D, 665A, 729E, 732C–D, 799E).

Divine guidance (811C) and mercy (875C) follow quite understandably from the view of God as omnibenevolent and as resolute in the path of justice, such that God should not be seen as amenable to bribes or flattery, as were the Homeric gods and goddesses. To be divine is to be as good as possible (899B); this includes genuine concern with the plight of creatures

(885D, 887B, 899D), in partial contrast to Aristotle's unmoved mover(s), whose supposed perfection would be compromised if they contemplated anything other than themselves. Perfect goodness (*pasan areten*—900D), superlative (*aristous*) goodness (901E), or an all-good being (902C) require not only cosmic order, in general. These also require a concern for, but not absolute control over, the details (900B, 900E, 901A, 902A, 903B, 904A–B, 905D, 906A, 907A; also see *Epinomis* 980D, 988B).

Chapter Four

Dipolar Theism

Introduction

In this chapter I would like to finish my treatment of the *concept* of God so as to move to Plato's arguments for the *existence* of God in the following chapter. Getting clear on the concept of God makes the effort to argue for the existence of God more likely of success. That is, an incoherent concept of God makes it difficult, or even impossible, to argue for the existence of a divine being-in-becoming. Along the way I will argue that confusion has arisen historically regarding Plato's view of God because scholars have generally not noticed the following ironic shift: Plato is famous for a dipolar categorical scheme, wherein form is contrasted to matter and being is contrasted to becoming, but he ends up with a cosmological monism wherein the divine animal (the World Soul) includes all; Aristotle, by way of contrast, is famous for a monopolar categorical scheme of embodied form, yet he ends up with a cosmological dualism more severe than anything found in Plato's dialogues. This is because Plato's theism does not involve an unmoved mover or unmoved movers that are pure actualities that transcend altogether the clash of potentialities found in the natural world of becoming.

Dipolar Theism

In this section of the chapter I will use the term *God* to refer to the supremely excellent or all-worshipful being. A debt to St. Anselm is evident in this preliminary definition. It closely resembles St. Anselm's "that than which no greater can be conceived." However, the ontological argument is not what is at stake here. Even if the argument fails, which both Hartshorne and I would doubt (and perhaps Plato, as we will see in the following chapter), the preliminary definition of God as the supremely excellent being, the all-worshipful being, or the greatest conceivable being seems unobjectionable. To say that God can be defined in these ways still leaves open the possibility that God is even more excellent or worshipful than our ability to conceive. This allows me to avoid objections from those who might fear that by defining God I am limiting God to "merely" human language and conception. I am simply suggesting that when we think of God we must be thinking of a being who surpasses all others, or else we are not thinking of God. Even the atheist or agnostic would admit this much. When the atheist says, "There is no God," she is denying that a supremely excellent, all-worshipful, greatest conceivable being exists.

The excellent-inferior contrast is the truly invidious contrast when applied to God.[1] If to be invidious is to be injurious, then this contrast is the most invidious one of all when both terms are applied to God because God is only excellent. God is inferior in no way. Period. To suggest that God is in some small way inferior to some other being is no longer to speak about God but about some being that is not supremely excellent, all-worshipful, or the greatest conceivable. The dipolar theist's major criticism of traditional Abrahamic theism is that it has assumed that all contrasts, or most of them, when applied to God are at least somewhat invidious, as in its preference for God as unchanging.

Let us assume that God exists. What attributes does God possess? Consider the following two columns of attributes in polar contrast to each other:

one	many
being	becoming
activity	passivity
permanence	change
necessity	contingency
self-sufficient	dependent
actual	potential
absolute	relative
abstract	concrete

Traditional Abrahamic theism tends toward oversimplification. It is comparatively easy to say that God is strong rather than weak, so in all relations

God is active, not passive. In each case, the traditional Abrahamic theist decides which member of the contrasting pair is good (on the left), then attributes it to God, while wholly denying the contrasting term (on the right). Hence God is one but not many, permanent but not changing, and so on. This leads to what Hartshorne calls the "monopolar prejudice."

Monopolarity is common to both traditional Abrahamic theism and pantheism, with the major difference between the two being the fact that traditional theism admits the reality of plurality, potentiality, and becoming as a secondary form of existence "outside" God (on the right), whereas in pantheism God includes all reality within itself. Common to both traditional Abrahamic theism and pantheism is the belief that the categorical contrasts listed above are invidious. The dilemma these two positions face is that either the deity is only one constituent of the whole (traditional Abrahamic theism)—a view that Plato, given his belief in the World Soul, should find problematic—or else the alleged inferior pole in each contrast (on the right) is illusory (e.g., Stoic pantheism).

However, this dilemma is artificial. It is produced by the assumption that excellence is found by separating and purifying one pole (on the left) and denigrating the other (on the right). That this is not the case can be seen by analyzing some of the attributes in the right-hand column. At least since St. Augustine, traditional Abrahamic theists have been convinced that God's eternity means not that God endures through all time but that God is outside of time altogether and is not, cannot be receptive to temporal change. St. Thomas Aquinas (following Aristotle, who was, it should be noted, the greatest predecessor to traditional Abrahamic theism) identified God as unmoved. Yet both activity and passivity can be either good or bad. Good passivity is likely to be called "sensitivity," "responsiveness," "adaptability," "sympathy," and the like. Insufficiently subtle or defective passivity is called "wooden inflexibility," "mulish stubborness," "inadaptability," "unresponsiveness," and the like. *Passivity* per se refers to the way in which an individual's activity takes account of, and renders itself appropriate to, the activities of others.[2] To deny God passivity altogether is to deny God those aspects of passivity that are excellences. Or, put another way, to altogether deny God the ability to change does avoid fickleness, but at the expense of the ability to benevolently react to the sufferings of others.

The terms on the left side also have both good and bad aspects. *Oneness* can mean wholeness, but also it can mean monotony or triviality. *Actuality* can mean definiteness, or it can mean nonrelatedness to others. What happens to divine concern when God, according to St. Thomas, is claimed to be pure actuality? God ends up caring for the world but is not intrinsically related to it, whatever sort of care that may be. Self-sufficiency can, at times, be selfishness.

The task when thinking of God is to attribute to God all excellences (left and right sides) and not to attribute to God any inferiorities (right and left sides). In short, excellent-inferior, knowledge-ignorance, or good-evil are invidious contrasts, but one-many, being-becoming, and the like are non-invidious contrasts. Consider the futility of treating good-evil as a noninvidious contrast; such an effort would involve a useless distinction between "good good" (a redundancy) and "evil good" (a contradiction). The inadequacies in traditional, monopolar theism in the Abrahamic religions have been pointed out by various mystics in the Abrahamic religions themselves in their critiques of the "God of the philosophers." Dipolar theism makes it possible to account for the religious experiences of the mystics, wherein God is moved by human love for the divine. That is, the God described by monopolar theists is not the only God of the philosophers.[3]

Within each pole of a noninvidious contrast (e.g., permanence-change) there are invidious or injurious elements (inferior permanence or inferior change) but also noninvidious, good elements (excellent permanence or excellent change). A dipolar, process theist such as Plato does not necessarily believe in two gods, one unified and the other plural. Rather, he believes that what are often thought to be contradictories or contraries are really mutually interdependent correlatives, as Hartshorne indicates: "The good as we know it is unity-in-variety or variety-in-unity; if the variety overbalances, we have chaos or discord; if the unity, we have monotony or triviality."[4]

Supreme excellence, to be truly so, must somehow be able to integrate all the complexity there is in the world into itself as one spiritual whole, as Plato would seem to agree in his doctrine of the World Soul. The word *must* indicates divine necessity, along with God's essence, which is to necessarily exist. The word *complexity* indicates the contingency that affects God through decisions made by self-moving creatures. In the traditional theistic view, however, God is identified solely with the stony immobility of the absolute, implying nonrelatedness to the world. God's abstract nature, God's being, may in a way escape from the temporal flux, but a living God is related to the world of becoming, which entails a divine becoming as well, if the world in some way is internally related to God as the divine animal. The traditional Abrahamic theist's alternative to this view suggests that all relationships to God are external to divinity, once again threatening not only God's concern for the world but also God's nobility. A dog's being behind a particular rock affects the dog in certain ways; thus this relation is an internal relation to the dog, but it does not affect the rock, whose relationship with the dog is external to the rock's nature.[5] Does this not show the superiority of canine consciousness, which is aware of the rock, to rocklike existence, which is unaware of the dog? Is it not therefore peculiar that God has been described solely in rocklike (Aristotelian) terms: pure actuality, permanence, having only external relations, unmoved, being and not becoming?

One may wonder at this point why monopolar theism has been so popular among theists (including, to a certain extent, Plato himself) when it has so many defects. Hartshorne suggests at least four reasons, none of which establishes the case for traditional, monopolar theism.

(1) It is simpler to accept monopolarity than dipolarity. That is, it is simpler to accept one and reject the other of contrasting (or better, correlative, noninvidious) categories than to show how each, in its own appropriate fashion, applies to an aspect of the divine nature. Yet the simplicity of calling God "the absolute" can come back to haunt the traditional Abrahamic theist if absoluteness precludes relativity in the sense of internal relatedness to the world.

(2) If the decision to accept monopolarity has been made, it is simpler to identify God as the absolute being than to identify God as the most relative. Yet this does not deny divine relatedness, nor that God, who cares for all, would therefore have to be related to all, or to use a roughly synonymous term, be relative to all. God may well be the most relative of all as well as the most absolute of all, in the sense that and to the extent that both of these are excellences. Of course, God is absolute and is relative in different aspects of the divine nature.

(3) There are emotional considerations favoring divine permanence, as found in the longing to escape the risks and uncertainties of life, as Plato himself indicates in the *Seventh Letter*. Yet even if these considerations obtain, they should not blind us to other emotional considerations, like those that give us the solace that comes from knowing that the outcome of our sufferings and volitions makes a difference in the divine life, which, if it is all good, will certainly not be unmoved by the suffering of creatures, even nonhuman creatures.[6]

(4) Monopolarity is seen as more easily made compatible with monotheism. Yet the innocent monotheistic contrast between the one and the many deals with God as an individual, not with the dogmatic claim that the divine individual itself cannot have parts or aspects of relatedness with the world.

In short, the divine being becomes, or the divine becoming is. God's being and becoming form a single reality, and there is no reason that we must leave the two poles in a paradoxical state. As Hartshorne puts the point, "There is no law of logic against attributing contrasting predicates to the same individual, provided they apply to diverse aspects of this individual."[7] The remedy for "ontolatry," the unqualified worship of being, is not the contrary pole, "gignolatry," the unqualified worship of becoming: "God is neither being as contrasted to becoming nor becoming as contrasted to being, but categorically supreme becoming in which there is a factor of categorically supreme being, as contrasted to inferior becoming, in which there is inferior being."[8] In dipolar theism the divine becoming is more ultimate than the divine being only for the reason that it is more inclusive, an inclusiveness that is essential to support Plato's defense of the World Soul. That is, to the extent that Plato adheres to monopolar theism he has a difficult time justifying his adherence to belief in God as the World Soul.

The theism toward which Plato points, and which I am defending through the thought of Hartshorne, is: (a) *dipolar* because excellences are found on both sides of the previously mentioned contrasting categories (i.e., they are correlative and noninvidious); (b) *neoclassical* because it relies on the belief that the classical or traditional Abrahamic theists (especially St. Anselm) were on the correct track when they described God as the supremely excellent, all-worshipful, greatest conceivable being, but the classical or traditional Abrahamic theists did an insufficient job of thinking through the logic of perfection; (c) *process* because it sees the need for God to become in order for God to be called "perfect", but not at the expense of God's always (i.e., permanently) being greater than all others; and (d) *panentheistic*, which, once again, literally means "all is in God." God is neither completely removed from the world—that is, is unmoved by it—as in Aristotelian theism, nor completely identified with the world, as in Stoic pantheism. Rather, God is (i) world-inclusive in the sense that God cares for all the world, and all feelings in the world are felt by God as the divine animal; and (ii) transcendent in the sense that God is greater than any other being, especially because of God's everlasting existence and supreme goodness. Thus, we should reject the conception of God as an unmoved mover not knowing the moving world (Aristotle); as the unmoved mover inconsistently knowing the moving world (classical or traditional Abrahamic theism); and as the unmoved mover knowing an ultimately unmoving, or at least noncontingent, world (Stoics, Spinoza, pantheism).[9]

Two objections may be raised by the traditional Abrahamic theist that ought to be considered. To the objection (found in the *Republic*) that if God changed God would not be perfect, for if God were perfect there would be no need to change, there is this reply: in order to be supremely excellent

God must at any particular time be the greatest conceivable being, the all-worshipful being. At a later time, however, or in a situation where some creature that previously did not suffer now suffers, God has new opportunities to exhibit divine, supreme excellence. That is, God's perfection does not merely allow God to change, but requires God to change.

God must be as great as possible at any particular time, or God would not be the greatest conceivable being. Yet new moments bring with them new possibilities for greatness, which God must realize in the best way possible if God is the greatest, or better, the unsurpassable. This means that God is greater than any being that is not God, but God can always surpass Godself. It does not mean that God's earlier existence was inferior, because it was at that earlier time the greatest conceivable existence, the greatest existence logically possible, and greater than any other being.

The other objection might be that God is neither one nor many, neither actual nor potential, and so forth, because no human concept whatsoever applies to God literally or univocally, but at most analogically. The traditional Abrahamic theist would say, perhaps, that God is more unitary than unity, more actual than actuality, as these are humanly known. Yet one wonders how traditional Abrahamic theists, once they have admitted the insufficiency of human conceptions, can legitimately give a favored status to one side (the left side) of conceptual contrasts at the expense of the other. Why, if God is more simple than the one, is God not also more complex, in terms of relatedness to the diversity of self-movers in the universe, than the many? Analogical predication and negative theology can just as easily fall victim to the monopolar prejudice as univocal predication. "To be agent and patient is in truth incomparably better than being either alone."[10] This is preeminently the case with God, and a human being is vastly more of both than a stone. Stones (when seen as insentient aggregates of sentient microconstituents) can neither talk nor listen, nor can they decide or appreciate others' decisions. God, on the dipolar Platonic view, is the greatest soul, the greatest self-mover, as well as the greatest reality in that God has the dynamic (but not omnipotent) power to affect all and to be affected by all.

REALITY AS DYADIC

We have seen that, like a child begging for both, Plato declares through the Eleatic Stranger in the *Sophist* (249D) that reality (as dynamic power) is both at once: the unchangeable and that which changes. This view has significant consequences for theism. In this dyadic reality can be distinguished a thing's abstract essence from its being-in-a-context-of-relations. Because our knowledge itself is relational, we can never fully know the essence of a thing, only an endless series of relations. This intimates how Plato still retains in the later dialogues the notion of separation (*chorismos*). This distinction between a thing's "in itself" and its "in relation" is expressed in the *Philebus* (23–25) as an indeterminate dyad. That is, in addition to the determination "given" to being by number, measure, and limit, there is also an unlimited factor of multiplicity. That the dyad is indeterminate perhaps indicates which side of the dyad (becoming) is more inclusive. The same point was hinted at—but confusedly so—as early as the *Republic* (501B), where the philosopher is supposed to keep one eye on the forms and the other on the images of these forms in "this" world.[11]

Hartshorne especially likes to use these Platonic insights to illustrate the aesthetic core of reality in that an individual is a functional unity-in-diversity, "so long as it endures at all." Plato's implied idea of beauty as integrated diversity and intensity of experience is truly metaphysical: "valid for any possible state of reality."[12] And as is perhaps the case in the indeterminate dyad of the *Philebus*, although there can be no assurance here, one pole in the dyad is more inclusive than the other. (We will see that this does not necessarily mean that there is no sense to be made of the notion of polar equality in dipolar theism.) It *is* clear to Hartshorne that dipolarity can be traced back to Plato, and this dipolarity is manifest in all reality, supremely so in God.[13] Each category and its contrary (e.g., being and becoming, unity and diversity, etc.) admits of a supreme case or a supercase. This is true whether we speak univocally or analogically about God. Therefore we are left with either two supreme beings or one supreme being with two "really distinct aspects." Only an overly literal interpretation of the *Timaeus* would allege that Plato took the first option. Relying on Cornford, Hartshorne holds that Plato took the second option, albeit vividly presented in myth as if the first option were chosen.[14] Such is Plato's wisdom, never so bold as to give all the answers and always a source for continued philosophic conversation.

For the sake of argument, Hartshorne would drop his thesis regarding phases of Platonic development, discussed in the introduction to this book, but he refuses to give up the thesis that there are two facets in Plato's thought.[15] The first is a *diaeresis* of existence into the quantitative and the qualitative, the mutable and the immutable, or better, the material and the formal (or ideational). Both soul and God are put in the latter (immobile) pole of these pairs. However, in the second facet (or phase) of Plato's thought, motion is granted to soul, including the World Soul. The "real opposition" here is between dependent and independent mobility, between body (taken as an insentient aggregate of protosentient constituents) and soul (including divine soul). Within the World Soul there is a principle of immutability (in that the World Soul's existence cannot end if an orderly world continues to exist), a principle that characterizes (divine) soul per se in the first facet (or phase). This complex of opposed concepts is not simplified by reducing God to the idea of the good. Not even in the first facet (or phase) did Plato ever clearly make this equation.[16] Rather, the good, although it is not God, is nonetheless compatible with the rule of supreme being-in-becoming in that it is the most exalted intellectual content contemplated by God. In short, the conflict of opposing categories must, then, be viewed as inherent in the Platonic framework. Reality, including divine reality, is one, but this unity can only be discursively or metaphysically understood as two, like centripetal and centrifugal forces in equilibrium.

There are two principles upon which Plato's theology turns: the "pure being" of the forms and the "supreme mobility" of soul.[17] The unchanging deity (including such deity's knowledge of the forms) of the *Phaedo*, *Republic*, and parts of the *Parmenides* is the supreme instance of fixity; the self-moving deity of the *Phaedrus* and *Laws* is the supreme instance of mobility. Alluding to the aforementioned passage in the *Sophist* (to the effect that Plato, like an entreating child, says "Give us both"), Hartshorne claims that the two poles of Plato's theism are brought together with almost equal weight in the *Timaeus*. But the word *together* is problematic in that Plato mythically fixes the correlative categories in different beings, the Demiurge and the World Soul, with the latter seemingly providing an answer to the criticism of the *Parmenides* that an absolute God could not know or be related to the world. We have seen that Hartshorne is not alone in thinking that Plato's myths and images stand for his real interest: concepts.[18]

The path of much later philosophy was to seek consistency and to sacrifice one of these poles (usually divine becoming), and this path was in some ways encouraged by Plato himself in that the two poles cannot be related if both are considered concrete divine natures. This is why Hartshorne sees the Demiurge as an eternal aspect of the everlasting World Soul, that is, the rational aspect of the divine life.[19] And this is what he thinks Plato could or should have done, for if Platonism means anything it is that there are distinct levels of ontological abstractness. Relying on Harry Wolfson, Hartshorne thinks of eternity as the absence of temporal relations, hence God's eternal aspect cannot be concrete in that concrete things have temporal relations; yet the World Soul for the body of the world—the divine animal—is obviously concrete.

Hartshorne is confident that his treatment of the Demiurge and the World Soul follows from basic Platonic distinctions and that it continues the direction of Plato's logic in the *Timaeus*, which attempts to render consistent the inconsistent positions on God of the *Phaedo* and *Republic*, on the one hand, and the *Phaedrus*, on the other. This is not to suggest that all of the threads in Plato's view of God have been picked up, even by Hartshorne. For example, we have seen that Plato sometimes multiplies gods into a pantheon of astral spirits, but these are mythical expressions that have seldom detained philosophers. Also, in the *Laws* the relation of self-motion to fixity is confusedly expressed in the figure of circular motion, and so on. But even a multiplication of astral spirits is not incompatible with a monotheistic intent, for to call these "deities" or "gods" in a loose way is a passing concession to popular piety where precision is not sought. Monotheism is close to the surface of Plato's approach in that God is not posited by Plato as a mere fact to explain some other observed facts. Rather, God (specifically, the demiurgic aspect of God) must apprehend the entire realm of forms, for God is the very principle of order in the world, the means by which the totality of things is one cosmos, a *uni*verse.

God's immutability is inferred from God's perfection in the *Republic*. This ascendancy of the principle of fixity has been taken throughout most of the history of philosophy to be the Platonic view of God *simpliciter*. It is helpful to notice that the World Soul is the supreme example of soul, but it is not perfect if perfection entails immutability. Or, mythically expressed, the World Soul is merely the most perfect of created things. Absoluteness (or perfection, as traditionally conceived in the Abrahamic religions) only belongs to an abstract, eternal aspect of God, to God's essence rather than to God's concrete actuality. Hence, Hartshorne finds no fault with the view of perfection in the *Republic*, but he tries to place it within a more inclusive view of God.[20] If Plato is to be faulted, it is because his spokesman in the *Republic* misleadingly talks of a being—instead of a mere abstract aspect of a being—so "perfect" that it could not change for the better or worse. That Hartshorne is not imposing his dipolar view on Plato is supported by the following consideration. If God were an *ens realissimum*, a most real being that could not change, either by improvement or by influence from others, God would come dangerously close to violating the definition of real being as dynamic power in the *Sophist*.[21] "The absolutely insensitive is the absolutely dead, not the supremely alive. The Platonists (perhaps not Plato) are blind to this truth."[22]

The two "Gods" of the *Timaeus* (the creator God and the created God—the Demiurge and the World Soul, respectively) are aspects of one and the same deity. The *uni*verse as an animate and rational effect is superior to all other effects "as the whole or inclusive effect is superior to parts or included effects."[23] But as in the *Republic* (381B), God is in every way the best possible (*ta tou theou pantei arista echei*). It is for this reason that Plato does not think that certain things are shameful in God merely because they are shameful in human beings. Rather, anything less than the best possible is shameful in God because it is incompatible with the divine nature itself. And "best possible" has implications not only for ethical issues, but also for God's knowledge of the forms. Mathematical forms are not, on Hartshorne's interpretation of Plato, directly pictorial or imaginable. Lines, for example, are only intuited as ideal limits such that "even omniscience would have them as data only in a very special way," which is still compatible with the view that God is the measure of perfection in the world.[24]

Hartshorne spent a great deal of his career criticizing the Neoplatonic and medieval worship of being as opposed to becoming—"a doctrine riddled with antinomies"—a worship largely due to the influence of Parmenides on Plato and to the assumption that such influence constitutes Plato's entire philosophy. Hartshorne criticizes most interpreters of Plato in assuming that Plato's last word on God was that in the *Republic* to the effect that God, being perfect, cannot change. To a lesser extent he also criticizes Plato himself for going so far down this road before realizing that "an absolute maximum of value *in every conceivable respect*, does not make sense or is contradictory."[25] Like the "greatest possible number," "absolute maximum value" can be uttered but does not say anything if finite beings contribute something to the greatness of God as they do to the supreme memory of the World Soul.

The meaning usually assigned to Plato's theory of forms was really born in the first book of Aristotle's *Metaphysics*, according to Hartshorne. Hence it is implausible to think that the greatest problem in Plato's cosmology is this theory of form, but rather it is that of sufficiently grasping the functions of soul as both receptive and creative and the related problems of understanding internal and external relations and how the soul interacts with body.[26] Plato's analysis of becoming remains incomplete (see *Sophist* 248–49) because if knowing something is to change that something, as we have seen Plato sometimes indicate, then past events go on changing when we think about them. Plato probably entertained this idea (that knowing something changes it) as a reaction against the opposite view that the past completely determines the present in souls as in bodies. The self-motion of soul must mean that the soul originates change, which is at least compatible with the view that necessary, although not sufficient, causal

conditions are inherited from the past. The soul does not merely trans-
mit tendencies from the past nor just receive them, as in bodies. It is no
stretch of the imagination to say that Plato anticipated the process transcendental "creativity" (once again, see *Laws* 892A, 896C, 899C, 959A; and
Epinomis 988D).[27]

For both Plato (perhaps not Plato*ism*) and Aristotle the abstract must
somehow be embodied in concrete reality. This embodiment is primarily in
God's thoughts for Plato. For Aristotle it is either *in re* (embodied in a material thing) or *post rem* (abstracted in the mind of a knower). So for Plato and
Aristotle no particular concrete entity is required by the abstract entity. A
"necessarily instantiated attribute could be clearly nonidentical with its
instances, and yet in its very being, as an attribute, instantiated somehow."[28]

But there is a difference of emphasis in the two thinkers, with Aristotle
developing a single categorical scheme of embodied form or substance
instead of Plato's dipolarity. Paradoxically, however, from this emphasis on
substance Aristotle ultimately constructs a more vicious dualism than any ever
envisaged by Plato, in that Aristotle's divinity is a completely self-sufficient
entity separated from all change and multiplicity. Painting with a rather wide
brush, the Hartshornian view seems to be that Plato's cosmology of psychical
monism can only be understood and explained through a dipolar categorical
scheme, whereas Aristotle's troublesome cosmological dualism (which historically gave rise to all of the—seemingly insoluble—problems of traditional Abrahamic theism) is elaborated through a monopolar scheme
favoring substance.[29]

Some Texts

In addition to some crucial texts treated above (e.g., *Sophist* 249D; *Philebus*
23–25), there are many others that support the case in Plato's dialogues for
the claims that reality is dyadic and that God's nature is dipolar. Many
scholars have been quick to note those places in the dialogues where Plato
flirts with ontolatry, the worship of being as opposed to becoming. Some
familiar texts come to mind. In the *Phaedo* (80A–B) the character Socrates
holds that it is the nature of the divine to rule and direct rather than to be
subject and serve. (This leads one to wonder if there is a variety of divine
passivity in Plato's dialogues that does not make God subject to the creatures and servile; I will return to this worry momentarily.) This facet
of Plato's view requires that there be something invariable (*homoiotaton*)
and indissoluble (*adialyto*) in God. Likewise in the *Republic* the character

Socrates urges that the healthiest and the strongest is the least altered, that which abides forever and which is incapable of change (*me metaballein*—380E, 381B–C, 381E, 382E; also see *Third Letter* 351B–C).

The principle of divine fixity, which exerted a tremendous influence not only over Aristotle but also over the Abrahamic religions,[30] admittedly finds its way into several of the later dialogues. In a startling passage in the *Theaetetus*, the character Socrates says that "these three doctrines coincide—the doctrine of Homer and Heraclitus and all their tribe that all things move like flowing streams, the doctrine of Protagoras … that man is the measure of all things, and Theaetetus' conclusion that, on these grounds, it results that perception is knowledge" (160D–E). Not surprisingly, this veiled criticism of Heraclitean thought is followed by a statement of admiration for his apparent opposite, Parmenides (183E). In the *Philebus* the character Socrates even suggests that becoming takes place with a view to the being of this or that, with a view to that which is unchanged (54C, 58A, 59C). To be self-sufficient (*autarkes*) is more excellent than lacking something that is required, as is also indicated in the *Timaeus* (33D, 47C). There is something inherently perilous about change, from the perspective of divine fixity (*Laws* 797D; also see *Epinomis* 982D–E, 985A). That is, the doctrine of divine being or completeness is encouraged by Plato himself when certain tendencies in his dialogues are emphasized without the reticulative effort to understand other (gignolatrous) tendencies.[31]

Later in this text we will consider passages from Plato's dialogues that flirt not with ontolatry but with its opposite, gignolatry, the worship of becoming. What are we to make of these contrasting tendencies in Plato? Of course one response would be to say that there simply is no Platonic philosophy, that the dialogues, when seen as dramas, exhibit contrasting tendencies that are not to be reconciled. On this view, any apparent conflicts in or among Platonic dialogues are material not so much for philosophic explication and analysis but for rhetorical examination. But if we were to attempt to logically reconcile the contrasting tendencies toward both ontolatry and gignolatry, is the situation really hopeless, as many scholars assume in thinking that the two columns of divine attributes are contradictory, rather than correlative? I think not. There is a way to reconcile the exaltation of both being and becoming, especially in the later dialogues, in terms of Hartshorne's distinction between divine *existence* and divine *actuality*. The former concerns the mere fact of God's existence, whereas the latter concerns how God exists or the mode of God's existence.[32]

Given this distinction, one is tempted to say that when the topic of conversation is God's bare existence, one can legitimately claim that God is unchanged, self-sufficient, invariable, indissoluble, and abides forever, as we have seen described earlier. There is no changing the fact that God always exists. However, when we consider divine actuality, the mode of God's existence or how God exists, it makes sense to describe God in terms of becoming and change, as we will see. Just as I constantly change, yet retain a stable identity as "Dan" throughout these changes (see *Symposium* 207D–E), analogously God everlastingly (or sempiternally) changes from moment to moment as a result of God's omnibenevolent and omniscient relationships with creatures yet retains a stable identity or permanent being as "God" throughout these preeminent changes.

Of course I am not claiming that Plato is entirely clear regarding divine being and becoming in the later dialogues. In fact, at one point the character Socrates in the *Theaetetus* (195C) confesses that, concerning some of the very issues with which I am concerned in the present chapter, he is "indeed garrulous—what else can you call a man who goes on bandying arguments to and fro because he is such a dolt that he cannot make up his mind and is loath to surrender any one of them?" We are once again reminded here of the crying child of the *Sophist* who wants both being and becoming. It is process philosophers who have spent the greatest effort trying to decipher how we can have both in a consistent manner. God's being refers to an abstract feature that applies to all of the concrete moments of becoming in the divine life.

At several points in the later dialogues the concern for divine being and divine becoming interpenetrate. Previously we have seen that in the *Theaetetus* (160D–E) the character Socrates offers a veiled criticism of the thought of Heraclitus that all things move like flowing streams, a criticism that makes sense if what it means to be a follower of Heraclitus is to deny the enduring, abstract feature or identity of (i.e., the being of) *a* thing in flux. But each being nonetheless is in flux, hence later in this dialogue some sort of rapprochement is reached with Heraclitus (179D): we are caught between both Parmenidean being and Heraclitean flux (179D–81A, 182C).

Throughout Plato's later dialogues the flirtation with gignolatry, and not only the flirtation with ontolatry, is evidenced. But even in the *Cratylus* (421B) we learn from the character Socrates that the etymology of *aletheia* (truth) involves not Heideggerian lack of concealment but rather a divine wandering (*theia ale*) or a divine motion.[33] God is moved by, or is at least pleased by, the creatures (*Phaedrus* 273E, 274B). Plato is correct, however, to criticize the fickleness of the Homeric gods and goddesses. His replacement view, given the evidence of divine omniscience and omnibenevolence treated in the previous chapter, seems to be that God *always responds* to the world by means of preeminent divine knowledge and good-ness (both words need emphasis). Plato's concern at *Phaedo* (80A–B) can be met: divine passivity concerns the actuality of God rather than the existence of God. The divine existence is not in any sense dependent on any particular creatures.

The prominence of divine motion in the later dialogues is due to the prominence of soul in these dialogues, with *soul* defined as "self-motion," especially in the *Phaedrus* and *Laws* X. Inactivity is inimical to soul; motion is its defining feature (see *Theaetetus* 153C). Soul in general (presumably including divine soul, the World Soul, or the divine animal) is characterized by great vitality (*ischyron*—*Phaedo* 95C; also see *Euthydemus* 302E). Indeed, in the *Cratylus* (399D) psyche is meant to express the source of, and the con-tinuing dynamic force behind, life. That is, soul is not a reified substance: rather it works (*Republic* 353D), it has power (*dynamin*—*Republic* 430B, 518C, 534C) and impulse (*hormen*—*Philebus* 35D) in its union with body to form a single compound (*eis mian amphotera krasin ienai*—*Philebus* 47C). Plato sounds surprisingly hylomorphist here, just as he does in the doctrine of the World Soul, where God is the soul for the body of the world. That is, Plato is surprisingly closer to cosmological hylomorphism than Aristotle, whose transcendent unmoved movers can only with great difficulty (actually, I think that the task is impossible) be related to the natural body of the world (also see the aforementioned passages: *Laws* 899C; *Epinomis* 980D, 983B, 988D). On this reading of Plato and Aristotle, medieval Aristotelianism was inconsistent in attributing omniscience to a wholly independent deity.[34]

Ivor Leclerc agrees that acting (*energeia*—not surprisingly, the etymo-logical root of our word *energy*) is a fundamental factor in what is accepted by Plato as *to pantelos on*: a complete or real being. And Leclerc thinks that Aristotle, at least, was correct to reject, if Plato himself did not do so (I think that he did), the idea that "the good itself" (*auto to agathon*) could be a self-subsistent being. Rather, along with the Neoplatonic and early Christian interpretation of Plato, the form of the good is an item (albeit an item of highest importance) in the divine psyche. If Whitehead is less convinced than Hartshorne that Plato got the forms into flux, as is alleged by Julius Bixler, then this lack of confidence in Plato's ability to do so seems to be the result of Whitehead's reticence to defend, along with Plato and Hartshorne, the belief in God as the dynamic soul for the body of the world.[35]

When a soul knows or is known, we learn from the Eleatic Stranger (presumably Plato) in the *Sophist* (248E–49D), the soul cannot remain changeless. That is, change is real on the definition of being in the *Sophist* that was explored in chapter 2. Reality embraces both rest and motion, hence both Parmenides and Heraclitus are partially correct and partially incorrect (250B, 252A, 252E–53A). As is well known, in the *Timaeus* (37D–39C) time is defined as, and is intended by God to be, a moving image of eternity. The passages in Plato's dialogues that associate God with eternity, I have alleged, can be rendered consistent with those that associate God with a concern for creatures, a concern or providence wherein God is moved by the plight of the creatures (see, e.g., *Laws* 905D, 931A–E; also see *Eighth Letter* 353B). The world process (*geneseos*) surely contains mortal beings, but for a religious believer such as Plato it also contains (or better, is contained in) an everlasting, besouled divinity (see *Epinomis* 977E).

Plato's definition of being as dynamic power in the *Sophist*, and the evidence in favor of his panpsychism or hylomorphism (rather than materialism or dualism) in the *Philebus*, *Laws*, and *Epinomis*, lead one to take seriously Hartshorne's interpretation of Plato to the effect that the zero of activity, including divine activity, cannot be distinguished from the zero of actuality. The connotations of "Platon*ism*" are far from Plato's mature thought. (It should be clear by now that I accept the Neoplatonic view or the view of Platon*ism* that forms are intradeical, but I reject the Neoplatonic view or the view of Platon*ism* that tends toward ontolatry.) Whitehead goes so far as to claim that the vibratory account of the universe found in contemporary relativity and quantum theories would have surprised Plato less than it would have surprised Newton. Hartshorne puts the point regarding Plato's comfort with a vibrating process view in the following forceful terms: "Plato, in his post-*Republic* maturity, transcended this knee-jerk eternalism, which was already in Parmenides and Zeno. Time is what we know; we had better be modest about our ability to absolutely negate it and have even a vestige of meaning left."[36]

Chapter Five

Arguments for the Existence
of God

INTRODUCTION

Now that my extended treatment of the Platonic concept of God is in place
(including considerable attention paid to God's *actuality*—how God exists
or the mode of God's existence), it is appropriate to explicate at this point the
Platonic case for the *existence* of God. Two arguments can be distinguished:
an implied version of the ontological argument in the *Republic* and explicit
versions (indeed the first developed versions) of the cosmological argument
in the *Laws* and the *Timaeus*. By the end of this chapter the rationality of
religious belief on a Platonic footing will be in place. We will see that these
two arguments for the existence of God are related to the Platonic concept
of 'divine actuality' as I have explicated it throughout the book.

THE ONTOLOGICAL ARGUMENT

Mattias Esser seems to be accurate in his judgment that no one before
St. Anselm explicitly defends the ontological argument.[1] A consideration of
the famous divided line in books 6 and 7 of the *Republic*, however, shows
that the argument is found in Plato in at least an implicit way. The divided
line establishes an epistemological/metaphysical hierarchy "whose supreme
rule is that verification is always from above, never from below."[2] The
opposite procedure (from below) is examplified by early logical empiricists
such as Russell and Carnap, whose reductive analysis of compound sentences terminates in so-called protocol sentences (denoting the sensory
atoms of Hume) such as "red here."

For example, the lowest level of the divided line is *eikasia*, which is usually translated as "imagination." The objects of such an operation clearly are images, but Plato indicates that these objects are not verified from below, in empiricist fashion, for if they were so verified universal skepticism would result, due to the fleeting character of images. The next highest level is *pistis* or "belief" (which, together with *eikasia*, exhaust the world of *doxa* or "mere opinion" concerning becoming). It is easy to misunderstand the character Socrates (Plato's presumed spokesperson) here. In fact, Plato's own language abets this possible misunderstanding. One gets the impression that the objects of *pistis* are sensible things, which might lead some to mistakenly assume a perceptual realism that is foreign to Plato. Beliefs at this level of the divided line are not so much about the data of the senses as they are about the causes of such effects. As Eslick insightfully puts the point:

> The beliefs we form even about the physical world are trans-
> empirical. ... Their truth or falsity must be determined on a higher level
> still. In any case the physical feelings ("events" would be more accurate,
> since for Plato, with his Heraclitean heritage from Cratylus, the physical
> world is in process) are themselves only images, moving images of eter-
> nal [or better, everlasting] spiritual realities.[3]

In order to confirm or falsify beliefs, one needs to do so from above in the divided line passage of the *Republic*. That is, one needs to cross over from the world of becoming to the world of being, as known by way of *dianoia* or "hypothetical understanding." Thinking by way of hypotheses is primarily examplified for Plato by the mathematical sciences (arithmetic, plane geometry, solid geometry, harmonics, and astronomy). The necessities discussed and demonstrated in these sciences remain hypothetical, involving an if-then connection in which the "if" clause cannot be eliminated. Further, dianoetic scientific demonstration can be either synthetic (where one begins with the first principles of the science—definitions, common notions, postulates—then moves downward deductively to theorems) or analytic (where instead of moving from hypothetical cause to effect, one moves in the reverse direction from effects to hypothetical cause).

To use Eslick's language, the base metals of synthesis and analysis on the level of *dianoia* are transmuted into the gold of *noesis* by an intellectual intuition of the form of the good in book 7.[4] If one has had such an intuition, the hypotheses of the mathematical sciences are destroyed in the sense that they lose their hypothetical character and are seen as necessary consequences of the unhypothetical first principle.

An insightful article by J. Prescott Johnson is helpful at this point. Johnson understands the Platonic principle that verification comes from above, not from below, to amount to an ontological argument for the necessary existence of the form of the good. Although Johnson does not discuss the relationship between the form of the good and God, if there is legitimacy to the neoplatonic and early Christian view that forms are items in God's mind (as I have defended this thesis above), then an argument for the necessary existence of the form of the good would, in effect, be an argument for the necessary existence of God.[5]

On Johnson's interpretation, the supreme formal reality is not to be treated as a mere hypothesis in that it is needed as a principle of order for all of the lesser forms. Knowledge of the form of the good requires no assumptions or hypotheses, nor does it rely on the use of images, as does *dianoia*. To use contemporary language, this knowledge is strictly a priori and necessary. No merely contingent existence could be thus known.[6] *Dianoia* is incapable of yielding incorrigible knowledge both because it begins with an unsubstantiated hypothesis and because it relies on at least partially distorting images.

Noesis, however (sometimes called "knowledge"—*episteme*—or dialectic—*dialektike*), is a mode of cognition that may start from provisional knowledge of the hypothesis, but it ends with "certain knowledge of the ultimate principle which exists with necessity. This principle, ultimate and unconditional, Plato calls the 'unhypothesized beginning' (*archen anhypotheton*)."[7] The anhypotheton is the form of the good or the sun in the famous similes of the cave and the sun. Unfortunately, no explicit description is given in the *Republic* concerning the process by which *noesis* moves from hypotheses to the anhypotheton, so any effort to understand this transition involves a certain amount of risky scholarly speculation. This is where Johnson is tremendously helpful. It is clear that the noetic move *is* a mode of cognition. In the following lines Johnson makes it clear why it is appropriate to see the ontological argument implied in Plato:

> The anhypotheton, or the unhypothesized, is the unconditioned. But if the anhypotheton is merely and only a conceptual object, an epistemological construct, it is dependent upon conditions. ... Thus the anhypotheton is either nothing at all—not even thinkable—or it is ontologically real as independent of all extraneous conditions, including the conditions of thought. Since, however, the anhypotheton is thinkable ... it is clear that the anhypotheton is the ontologically real being necessarily existing in its possession of extra-epistemological reality.[8]

It is not my intention to argue in detail for the soundness of the ontological argument. Rather, my aim here is to claim both that the argument is
implied in Plato and that, on a Platonic basis, one can defend one's belief in
the existence of God not only through the cosmological argument but also
through the ontological argument. It is not surprising that most philosophers in the history of the discipline who have been called "Platonists" have
also been defenders of the ontological argument and of the principle that
verification is from above rather than from below, as empiricists suggest, by
way of contrast. The above quotation from Johnson makes it clear that, on
a Platonic basis, to claim that the anhypotheton is contingent is a contradiction in terms: to say that the anhypotheton depends for its existence on
certain limiting conditions or hypotheses is to contradict oneself.

As Hartshorne has repeatedly emphasized throughout his career, on the
basis of the ontological argument we can conclude that God's existence
(including God's understanding of the form of the good) is either impossible or necessary in that the only remaining alternative in modal logic (i.e.,
the contingent existence of God) is contradictory regarding the greatest
conceivable. Hence the argument is best seen as suggesting that if God's
existence is possible, then it is necessary. Johnson, as is seen in the above
quotation, is confident that we *can* have a concept of the form of the good
(and, by implication, of God); hence God is possible, despite the fact that
there is evidence in the text (509B) of a certain apophatic tendency in Plato
wherein the form of the good transcends essence in dignity and power.

In any event, the cosmological argument in the *Laws* and the *Timaeus*
can be used to supplement the implicit ontological argument in the *Republic*
in the following way: the cosmological argument makes it clear that we *can*
get a legitimate concept of God. This concept facilitates the following
choice before us as a result of the ontological argument: either God's existence
is impossible or necessary; but it is not impossible (as in the cosmological
argument); hence it is necessary. The two arguments, Hartshorne thinks, are
like mutually reinforcing (Peircian) strands in a cable that lead to an overall
or global argument for the existence of God that is quite strong.[9]

THE COSMOLOGICAL ARGUMENT

It is with good reason that John Baillie refers to Plato as the father of natural
theology.[10] His pioneering arguments for the existence of God, in particular,
and their influence on the Abrahamic religions, especially Christianity, are
noteworthy.[11] These arguments include an implicit version of the ontological

argument, as we have seen, as well as cursory versions of a teleological argument and an argument from consent (see *Laws* 886). The latter amounts to not much more than an *argumentum ad populum*: because people (Greeks and non-Greeks) are religious believers, religious belief is authenticated. It is easy to see the major defect in this argument in that people could be wrong. However, it is worth noting that facile agnosticism and atheism can be partially counteracted by appeal to an argument from consent: because most people are religious believers of some sort, one should be skittish about any kneejerk agnosticism or atheism that is itself not rationally defended.

The teleological argument offered by Clinias (nb., *not* by Plato's presumed spokesperson, the Athenian) in *Laws* X is a bit more sophisticated than the argument from consent but not much so (886, 889–90). Atheists, the objects of the Athenian's critique in *Laws* X, will say that heavenly bodies are only earth and stone; the order that we perceive in the natural world is largely due to chance combination of basic elements (earth, air, fire, water). The same will be claimed by the atheist regarding plants and animals. That is, on the atheist view, the gods are human inventions and hence may be disregarded. Because the teleological argument is not of much use in responding to atheism, the Athenian proposes a stronger argument, the cosmological one.[12]

There are actually several versions of a cosmological-type argument in Plato's dialogues. (Despite the fact that the cosmological argument is presented by the Athenian as stronger than the teleological one, William Lane Craig thinks that the presence of teleology in the universe provides the foundation for Plato's theism.) I will examine two versions. The first is in the *Laws* X (893B–99C) and is seen by the Athenian (and presumably by Plato) as an adequate refutation of atheism. In formal outline, this version (which is similar to cruder, earlier versions in the *Phaedrus* 245–46 and in Xenophon's *Memorabilia*) looks like this, on Craig's interpretation:

1. Some things are in motion.
2. There are two kinds of motion: communicated motion and self-motion.
3. Communicated motion implies self-motion because:
    a. things in motion imply a self-mover as their source of motion
        i. because otherwise there would be no starting point for the motion; and
        ii. because things moved by another imply a prior mover;
    b. if all things were at rest, only self-motion could arise directly from such a state:
        i. because a thing moved by another implies the presence of another moving thing;
        ii. but this contradicts the hypothesis.

4. Therefore, the source of all motion is self-motion or soul.
5. Soul is the source of astronomical motion because:
   a. the heavens are in motion; and
   b. soul is the source of all motion.
6. There is a plurality of souls because:
   a. there must be at least one to cause good motions;
   b. there must be at least one to cause bad motions.
7. The soul that moves the universe is the best soul because the motions of the heavens are good, being regular and orderly like those of the mind.[13]

With this proof argumentative theism becomes an explicit part of philosophy. God is claimed to be the *arche kineseos*, the source of motion (Taylor interestingly translates *kinesis* and its cognates as "process").[14] The first step in the argument indicates its *a posteriori* character. A key moment of the argument comes at the third step, where it is claimed that communicated motion implies self-motion. Without a first mover there would be no source or starting point of change. Plato does not defend this claim with any argumentation, however, in that an infinite regress alternative is taken by Plato to be self-evidently ridiculous, according to Craig. Later defenders of the cosmological argument will argue that if the series of movers is the datum to be explained, then to posit an infinite regress of such movers in effect constitutes a begging of the question. That is, to posit an infinite regress of movers without a first mover is to explain away the need for a real explanation or ground or beginning.

The question arises as to whether by "beginning" Plato means a temporal starting point or an ultimate source. The second alternative is clearly intended in that there is no evidence in the text that Plato saw a problem with a soul's always moving a body around in space. (Further, it seems that an omnipotent God is required for a temporal starting point in creation *ex nihilo*, and the evidence against divine omnipotence in Plato is considerable, as we have seen in chapter 2.) As before, God (including the forms in the demiurgic mind) and the natural world both appear to be everlasting in Plato. God or the best soul is not temporally prior to other movers but logically or causally prior. As Craig puts the point, "if one were to remove the ultimate source of motion going on right now, then the motion would cease, and everything would be frozen into immobility."[15] We have also seen that *psyche* must sometimes be translated as "mind," rather than as "soul" or "life," when it is considered that the divine soul (in its demiurgic function) apprehends the abstract objects of the intellect, the forms, as detailed by Craig, Grube, and Solmsen alike.[16]

It seems that Plato emphasizes the first soul as the source of astronomical motion in step five because astronomy is the science that would awaken (agnostic or atheistic) human beings to their "divine destiny," to use Skemp's language.[17] The first soul must be great enough to move the stars across the sky. More problematic is the idea that there is a plurality of souls/self-movers/gods in step six. The safest course is to say that there is evidence in the dialogues for both polytheism and monotheism, as we have seen. If I am correct in assuming that the former is not a viable option in contemporary philosophy (although this claim is by no means unproblematic),[18] we would be better served by concentrating on whatever light Plato could shed on monotheism. He does refer to the supremely good soul or the best soul (*aristen psychen*—897C) in the seventh step, by which I assume he means the best of many. Yet we have seen that the fact that the *uni*verse is an orderly whole, a cosmos rather than a pluriverse, indicates that monotheism is close to the surface of his writings even when he talks about the "gods." And we have seen that there is no reason to take Plato's mythic language to really refer to two deities, one good and one bad. Rather, as Grube claims, the concept of one God (*theos*) involves two aspects: the static in the midst of the dynamic.[19] As Craig puts the point regarding a famous debate on this topic between Taylor and Cornford (a debate that reached rapprochement): "Plato's lesser gods are all under the sovereignty of a single, supreme will and intelligence, which constitutes at least an implicit monotheism. To allow Plato to speak of God (with the capital letter) is to run much less risk of falsifying his thought than to call him a pagan polytheist."[20] Further, the plurality of gods in Plato's dialogues should have helped him to locate the source of evil in the world: not with an evil "God" but with a plurality of self-movers who get in each other's way.

God here in *Laws* X is easily seen as the same God discussed in the *Timaeus*. In fact, the second version of the cosmological argument that I would like to isolate (which was presumably written earlier than and is less developed than the *Laws* version) is in the *Timaeus* (27 ff.). Geisler summarizes the salient points in this argument in approximately the following terms:

1. The *cosmos* would be chaos without forms (pure stuff without any structure).
2. Chaos (the formless) is evil and *cosmos* (the formed) is good, by definition.
3. All types of goodness in the world come from a good Former.
4. No Former can shape good things without the form of the good after which to pattern them.

5. The form of the good after which the changing sensible world is formed must be an unchanging intelligible pattern.

6. Therefore, there is both a Former of all good things in the world (the Demiurge) and the form of the good after which all good things are formed.[21]

We have seen that many scholars (Taylor, Solmsen, Grube, Cornford, Craig, etc.) see the World Soul as the logical product of Plato's uses of the cosmological argument, with the Demiurge an aspect of the World Soul associated as a literary device both with wisdom itself and with wise creative agency: the Demiurge is the figure representing reason in the World Soul. To put the issue in the terms of the *Sophist* (249A): *nous* must have *zoe*, and these two can exist together only in a soul. We have come a long way from the caricature of Plato's philosophy discussed by Charles Bigger, to the effect that Plato's treatment of the World Soul is more fitting for discussion in "the Tibetan Theosophical Society" than in a scholarly journal. Bigger's process interpretation of the World Soul helps to counteract this caricature.[22]

These two versions of the cosmological argument in Plato do not seek to demonstrate the necessary actuality of God, but the fact of God's existence as the only possible explanation of the world. Other hypothetical causes have to be excluded for the argument to be successful, which amounts to showing that an infinite regress of causes is impossible. To link this argument with the dipolar theism of the previous chapter, we should say along with Eslick that "the abstract necessity of God's existence (that the class of perfect being, unsurpassable by any other, cannot be null) does not determine the concrete *actuality* of such existence. The latter aspect, even of God, is contingent."[23]

That is, the argument leads us to infer the existence of God, but it does not necessarily lead us to Aristotle's or Thomas Aquinas' unmoved mover, rather to a Supreme Self-Mover. Plato's cosmological argument is a demonstration *quia*: moving from effects to cause by resting its case on the impossibility of an infinite regress of causes, which atheists defend. As Eslick puts the issue in his explication of Plato: "Life is *either* the product of a first principle of life, essentially living with a life not received from another, for which the name is *soul, or* it is an epiphenomenal by-product, the result of the chance arrangement of non-living materials. The first hypothesis is Plato's."[24]

We have seen the inadequacies of defending *simpliciter* the view of God's perfection as necessarily entailing immutability and of Plato as defending an aggressive version of apophaticism.[25] Whereas the first hypothesis of the *Parmenides* deals with a unity that is just one, simple, and without parts or change (a unity concerning which *nothing whatsoever* can be predicated), in the *Sophist, Timaeus,* and *Laws* we find that nothing—not even God—can either exist or be known all by itself, in isolation from all dependent relations on others. Divine being-in-becoming has *dynamis,* both the power to make a living difference to others and the power to be influenced by living others.

USEFUL CONNECTIONS

In this final section of the chapter I would like to draw some useful connections: (1) between Plato's implicit use of the ontological argument in the *Republic* and the blended teleological/cosmological argument of the *Laws*; and (2) between all of his arguments for the existence of God and the other major facets of his theistic metaphysics, including the World Soul, the forms, and theodicy. This last concern is especially crucial when it is considered that it is often traditional theism's inability to account for evil in the world that gives rise to agnosticism and atheism.

Plato's treatment of the World Soul is not unrelated to his anticipation of the ontological argument. God's bare existence is quite abstract, as we have seen, about as noncompetitive as "reality as such." It has an infinite range of variations and flexibility. But God is not characterless or "flabby" because of God's actuality in some embodied state.[26] Hartshorne notes that there were atheists in Plato's day, and even before that (*Laws* 887C), so that Plato's teleological argument, blended with the cosmological argument, starts the important tradition of knowing how to rationally respond to the nonbelievers. Plato's use of what Hartshorne sees as this blended argument in *Laws* X shows both the importance of the World Soul and that Plato was "one of the most penetrating of all intelligences," a mind with "imaginative subtlety" that dwarfs his most famous followers.[27] Further, the blended argument is intended as a series of hints, to be filled in by the reader's meditations, which Hartshorne is obviously willing to do. But even though the argument is really an outline, it furnishes the material for an argument that is quite strong, he thinks.

Hartshorne's outline, which links the blended argument to a Platonic theodicy, looks something like this:

1. Psychical process or soul is the only self-explanatory process, the only self-determining type of change.

2. Order among souls, and hence in reality generally, can be explained only through a supremely good soul, which persuades the others to conform to its decisions.
3. Disorder and evil are not due to the supreme soul's decisions, but to the conflicting decisions of other souls.

Although Plato came too close to identifying disorder and evil (for Hartshorne partial disorder is needed to balance order so as to produce beauty—sheer order is not beautiful, but monotonous), his wisdom is seen when Hume and Kant suggest that the disorder in the world might be explained polytheistically. This is an extreme and inadequate way to put Plato's very point, if by "gods" is meant souls. Because the higher the consciousness the more "widely and abruptly" it can disagree with other consciousnesses that are its peers, a pantheon of gods would be even more in need of a single superior to understand the world as a cosmos than a plurality of earthly animals.

Hartshorne agrees with Burnet that Plato's greatest discovery regarding God does not concern the forms but rather concerns soul or psychical process. This discovery allows us to understand that the primordial and everlasting ideal for the cosmos—the form of the good—exists in the supreme soul; to realize that "creativity" is the true transcendental, which applies to creator and creature alike; to claim that cosmic order requires one soul to order the others, yet disorder does not require, as Plato sometimes indicates, one evil soul (e.g., a Satan), only a multiplicity of agents able to get in each other's way; and to urge that the traditional theistic "problem of evil" could not flourish in Plato's thought because God is not totally responsible for the world.[29] (Although Plato does waver between attributing evil to an Evil Soul, to "matter," or to the freedom of souls.)[30] Nor does Hartshorne think that it would be a good thing for God to be so responsible: beauty requires partial disorder, and cosmic creativity is a good thing.

This is no trivial attempt at theodicy. There are metaphysical reasons for these claims. From Plato Hartshorne has learned that every negation (relative nonbeing or otherness) implies an affirmation. There are no merely negative truths. To say that "divinity does not exist" is to say something positive about the reality whose existence is incompatible with God. Usually it is the positive existence of evil in the world that is assumed to be incompatible with (an omnipotent) God, but if there is no such incompatibility, then Plato's blended teleological/cosmological argument stands, as does the tragic view of life because there are pervasive elements of chance, partial disorder, and frustration in reality.

Plato's and Hartshorne's thoughts on the divine body are not just consequences of their use of the organic soul-body analogy to understand God. They are also logically entailed by their metaphysics, including their use of the ontological argument. Hartshorne has often claimed (contra Kant, et al.) that there are necessary truths concerning existence, as in "something exists." The futility of claiming that "there might have been absolutely nothing" is derived from Plato himself (and Bergson), who, when he commits parricide on father Parmenides in the *Sophist* (241–42), only admits the existence of relative nonbeing or otherness, not the existence of absolutely nothing, which would be a logical contradiction in that *it* would then be something.[31] Along with Plato and Spinoza, Hartshorne agrees that all determination is negation, but this inescapable element of negation is precisely Plato's form of otherness or relative nonbeing. The statement *absolutely nothing exists* could not conceivably be verified. That is, a completely restrictive or wholly negative statement is not a conceivable yet unrealized fact but an impossibility.[32] Particular bodies can pass out of existence (or better, into an other sort of existence), but the divine body of the universe itself has no alternative but to exist.

If one identifies the form of the good with God, then Plato in effect looks like a traditional Abrahamic theist, with God as both a necessary existent and a necessary actuality characterized by pure absoluteness. But, as we have seen, this is a difficult view to defend on textual grounds. If the form of the good is a necessary feature or idea in God, then God for Plato may well be absoluteness necessarily existent somehow, but with the particular actuality of God contingent and relative. It is this latter interpretation that Hartshorne adopts in an attempt to reconcile Johnson's insights regarding the ontological argument in the *Republic* and the *Timaeus*. What in Plato himself was probably an unresolved ambiguity regarding the relation between the form of the good and God—a wise restraint on Plato's part—tended in some of his followers to become a "premature and unwise" decision in favor of the first interpretation, hence the "fatal onesidedness" that has "exacted severe penalties" in the history of thought about God.[33]

The very notion of the Demiurge as a creator God presupposes modal concepts that make the ontological argument at least implicit in Plato. If the Demiurge's own existent reality actualized a potential that could have been unactualized, then the Demiurge is just as much in need of a creator as any other being. Thus the Platonic blended teleological/cosmological argument in *Laws* X "breaks down if Anselm's discovery is a mere sophistry."[34] Plato (or better, Platonism) misled Anselm at several points, as in assuming that reality does not admit of increase (consider, e.g., that we can always conceive of a greater for any conceivable number). It will not do to assume, as many followers of Plato have done, that deity's qualitative supremacy transcends magnitude altogether. Quantity may have a value that is not attainable without it, as in appreciating more moments of a creature's life rather than fewer. This defect is closely connected with the monopolar prejudice in favor of mere unity, as though absence of contrast could make sheer unity intelligible. A related Hartshornian criticism would apply to the Platonic vision of "absolute beauty," which is a contradiction in terms if in fact beauty entails variety, for "all possible variety" is full of mutual incompatibilities.[35]

All traditional, Abrahamic theists are Platonists, *in a certain sense*, in that they believe that "the universal principle of being can be a sort of superconcrete yet eternal reality," immune to becoming, but not an abstraction. They think that goodness itself is the most good thing, which exemplifies what Hartshorne calls the "homological fallacy": eternal principles (*logoi*) are in no way abstract or inferior to, but quite like concrete actualities. As should now be obvious, Hartshorne is not convinced that Plato himself committed this fallacy. Hartshorne does, however, argue against this "Platonizing" procedure, not Plato's own thought, in the following way: contingency is in the step from universal to particular, a step from the more abstract to the more concrete. Hartshorne realizes that the view that forms are not ultimately separable from concrete instances is "often termed the Aristotelian view." But the belief that universals must have some embodiment—say in a divine mind thinking them—can be fairly termed a "moderate Platonism," to use Hartshorne's language.[36]

The contrast between "predicates" and "exemplified predicates" is not the ground for contingency because of the priority that must be given to the latter. Some predicates must be exemplified, or there would be nothing to talk about. Rather, the ground of contingency is in the distinction between (a) specific predicates, which always involve mutual exclusiveness, competitive ways of instancing more general notions, alternative "determinates" under higher "determinables," and (b) generic predicates, which are less determinate. But only an "ultra-Platonic negation" would view forms as not specialized or concretized at all. The contingency of each step toward particularity does not mean that no definite step might have been taken but that "other *equally definite* steps" might have been taken. "Not even Plato" believed in the complete self-sufficiency of the abstract or universal. Plato was never "ultra Platonic."[37]

How do these considerations relate to the ontological argument? For Hartshorne the argument is valid only if the individuality of God is conceivable as a pure determinable that must be particularized and concretized somehow. God's bare existence is quite abstract, as we have seen, about as noncompetitive as "reality as such." It has an infinite range of variations and flexibility. But, once again, God is not characterless or flabby because of God's actuality in some embodied state. The definitive functions of deity are strictly universal and coextensive with modality as such: God is related actually to all actual things and potentially to all potential things. God is—because of the *Sophist*—influenced by and influences everything. Thus, modal coextensiveness is equivalent to the notion of the unsurpassable. The mistake of "Platonism" in the bad sense of the term is the notion that all beautiful things must preexist in the Absolute Form of Beauty, an ultimate determinable that somehow issues in determinations. But this is to deny any intelligible creativity, divine or creaturely. "To be creative is to add positive determinations to reality, to enrich the totality of things by new values." Hence the ultimate determinable is the supreme creativity, abstractly conceived. In the neoclassical, process, "moderately Platonic" use of Plato, we can see that Plato avoids not only the homological fallacy but also the formal fallacy whereby formal reality gives to concrete reality what formal reality itself lacks.[38]

The character Socrates in the *Republic* makes it clear that only a deranged person (*aner akribos*—573C) attempts to rule over the divine. Unlike Protagoras, Plato (through his spokespersons) is more than willing to "drag in" the divine in that we are not as wise as God, and we are in need of divine wisdom (*Theaetetus* 162C–D). This "dragging in" of the divine, however, relies on argument, rather than on the gullibility of simple minds that are persuaded of almost anything, even the belief that human beings sprang up out of teeth sown in the ground, as the Athenian notes in the *Laws* (663E–64A). Plato seems to have been ambivalent about this naive characteristic of simple minds, however: sometimes denigrating it, due to its inability to countenance a rational account, and sometimes praising it, because it issues in an unquestioned belief in God, rather than in atheism (679C, 948B).

Plato's preference seems to be for those who offer rational support for three crucial beliefs: that there is God, that God is mindful of us, and that God cannot be seduced away from the right path (*Laws* 907B, 966C–67D). And we have seen that the existence of evil does not threaten these beliefs, as it does traditional theism in the Abrahamic religions, where an omnipotent God, who omnisciently knows with absolute assurance and in minute detail what will happen in the future, should be called into question when evil appears. Surprisingly, Plato is somewhat aware of the theodicy problem as it is found in traditional theism in the Abrahamic religions, as when the character Socrates in the *Republic* is challenged to explain why the gods assign many good people misfortunes (364B). Plato's response, however, seems to be not to challenge the existence of God, nor is it to call into question divine omnibenevolence, but rather it is to avoid belief in the sort of divine omnipotence that is largely assumed without argument in traditional, Abrahamic theism.

Through the character Socrates in the *Theaetetus* (170A–B), Plato makes it clear that he is aware that there are some who passively wait for others to answer their ultimate questions for them. But this inactivity characterizes only some who believe in the existence of God. Further, in the presence of evil it is not deity that we should fault but either humanity or some inadvertent clash of self-movers (*Epinomis* 979B).

Chapter Six

Becoming like God

INTRODUCTION

In this final chapter of the book, I would like to make the case for Plato's theocentrism and for his belief that the *telos* of human life is to become as much like the divine as possible. In this effort I will be concentrating, as I have done throughout the book, on Plato's later dialogues. First, I will consider Robert Carter's thought-provoking thesis regarding Plato as a mystic on the evidence of certain middle dialogues. Then I will examine in detail crucial passages in the *Theaetetus* (176B–C) and *Timaeus* (90A–D), also treated in detail by David Sedley, Julia Annas, and others, to the effect that our goal in life should be to become as much like the divine as possible (*homoiosis theoi kata to dynaton*). In that this goal is common to almost all religious believers, Plato's approach to this topic should be of interest to contemporary religious believers in the Abrahamic religions, whether they be classical/traditional or neoclassical/process theists.

PLATO AND MYSTICISM

Because of the vagueness of the term *mysticism*, there is no general agreement regarding whether Plato was a mystic. At no point in the dialogues or in the letters do we have unambiguous evidence concerning Plato's own religious experiences, as we do concerning Socrates' experiences, as portrayed in the *Symposium* and elsewhere. That is, the issue to be explored in this section is the extent to which Plato's writings express a mystical philosophy or that advocate as a goal mystical unification with God.[1]

If we start a consideration of Plato's mysticism with William James' famous four criteria for mysticism in his *Varieties of Religious Experience*, some interesting results follow. James' four criteria are as follows: (1) ineffability; (2) noetic quality; (3) transiency; and (4) passivity.[2] One of the problems with these criteria is that everyday sense experiences meet three of the criteria (they yield knowledge, they are transient, and they find us receptive), as Walter Kauffman notices.[3] This leaves only ineffability as unique to mystical experience. On this limited basis, however, there are good grounds for seeing Plato's philosophy as mystical in that at several well-known passages a "final vision" is described as ineffable. For example, in the *Seventh Letter* (341C) Plato indicates that true knowledge cannot be put into words. Rather, after long interaction between teacher and pupil in a joint pursuit of wisdom, a sudden flash of insight can occur, like a fire that is carefully kindled. Or again, in the *Phaedrus* (276C–D) the character Socrates warns that written words only remind us of that with which writing is concerned. It is not that the ineffable cannot be expressed in words at all (in which case Plato's dialogues, myths, and symbols would be useless) but rather that it cannot be expressed *adequately* by any formulae or oral/written language.

Carter notices that the experiences described in the above two passages are both noetic in quality and they involve passivity (although one may actively work to be passively receptive to divine influence, on the analogy of actively working to hear a soft voice). In one sense, a mystical experience is transient, yet once attained it is difficult to revert to one's previous, lower sort of life. One cannot look at the light of the sun, as in book 7 of the *Republic* or have a vision of the form of beauty, as in the *Symposium*, for a long time, but when one returns to the cave of ordinary existence one's life is infused with the higher awareness made possible by the experience of this beautiful light. It is for this reason that Bergson was especially intent on calling into question the transiency of mystical experiences.[4]

In any event, a final vision (obviously not temporally final) or a mystical experience is different from everyday experiences in that such a final vision sets the philosopher apart from the rest of the population (*Phaedrus* 249D; also see the murder of the philosopher who returns to the cave in the *Republic*). More important for the purposes of the present book, if we define mysticism (as does W. T. Stace)[5] as a reticulative vision of the sense of the unity of the whole of things, then Plato's defense of the World Soul in several of the later dialogues, as detailed in chapter 1, is itself evidence of a mystical philosophy or an attempt to lead the philosopher to mystical union with God.

Skepticism regarding the claim that Plato's philosophy culminates in mystical experience seems to be based primarily on the fear that, if such a claim were true, Plato's commitment to reason would be severed. However, the mystical way that proceeds by stages from the darkness of the cave to the light of the sun, wherein the chains of the everyday world must be broken in order to experience the sudden awareness of the desired goal, the value of which can be expressed only partially, nonetheless requires reason to lead one to the final vision. On this interpretation, dialectic is not betrayed, but fulfilled, in mystical experience. Friedlander may be correct in saying that Plato's stress on the rational is unusual among mystics,[6] but the phenomenon is not unique. For example, St. Teresa of Avila brought St. John of the Cross to the Carmelite order precisely because he would bring intellectual rigor to the meditative lives of the Carmelite friars and nuns.

A related concern of those (like Friedlander) who are skeptical of the claim that Plato's philosophy is mystical rests on the assumption that mysticism requires that one despise the senses and hate the world. Platonic *askesis*, however, does not have to be seen in these terms in that the evidence of the dialogues of a certain hostility toward the senses does not necessarily indicate a desire to escape from the world but to transform it, or at least to transform our attitude toward it. In several dialogues, including the *Symposium*, the senses are given a crucial role to play in the effort to know the forms. Further, both the *Republic* and the *Laws* are presumably efforts to transform both the polis and the individual souls of those who reside in it. The way to respond to the worries of those who are skeptical of the claim that Plato's philosophy is mystical is to emphasize that, for Plato, philosophy is a way of life, rather than an intellectual effort alone, although it should also be emphasized that the intellect is the most important component in such a life. Ironically, given the fact that he was not a religious believer, a distinction from Bertrand Russell[7] is helpful in this regard: rational proofs for the existence of God, such as those explored in the previous chapter, give us knowledge of God by description, whereas mystical experience gives us knowledge of God by acquaintance.

Earlier in the book, in connection with Plato's flirtation with panpsychism, it was noted that in every besouled thing there is a spark of divinity. Because of this divine indwelling it makes sense that in the *Ion* and *Phaedrus* there is evidence of *enthousiasmos* or possession by deity and that at least some of the madness that this enthusiasm elicits can be put to philosophical use. Whitehead's distinction in *The Function of Reason* between the reason of Plato and the reason of Ulysses helps us here to better understand Plato: the latter sort of reason (or cunning) is shared with the foxes, he thinks, but Plato's reason directs us toward the divine. That is, a Platonic "complete understanding" is different from a Ulysseslike "immediate method of action."[8] Or again, in *Adventures of Ideas* Whitehead analogously distinguishes between a truly liberal, Platonic education, which includes a place for religion and religious experience, and a more technical sort of education.[9]

Another stumbling block for some interpreters arises when Plato's "final vision" (again, not in the sense of temporal finality) is compared to the "final vision" of other philosophers. Aldous Huxley's largely ignored distinction between apotheosis and deification can operate here as a helpful heuristic device.[10] The former occurs when a human soul is exalted and intensified to the point where the person ceases to be a mere human being and becomes godlike. By way of contrast, deification occurs when the human soul remains such but is more and more infused with the divine. The Eastern Orthodox concept of the process of *'theosis'* is closer to the meaning of deification than it is to the meaning of apotheosis. Likewise with respect to St. John of the Cross's notion of *endiosada*. In fact, Hazel Barnes interprets Platonic mysticism more in terms of deification than in terms of Homeric or Nietzschean apotheosis.[11] On her interpretation, Nietzsche's *ubermensch* is the culmination of the search for apotheosis. At the other extreme, she thinks, is Huxley's belief that life in this world is worthless in that ultimate reality is radically other. Seen in this light, Platonic mysticism is characterized by moderation and a harmonious relation between "this" human world and "that" divine one. Seeing Plato as moderate in this regard will help us to respond a bit later to some of Annas' queries regarding Plato's stance.

I agree with Barnes that Platonic mysticism or deification is not to be associated with world denial. Indeed, the panentheistic belief in the World Soul seems to indicate world deification without the usual determinism and leveling effect of pantheism. It is true that in Plato's middle dialogues (especially in the *Phaedo*, where there is an incentive provided by hemlock for Socrates—or for the character Socrates—to separate his soul from his body) can be found a certain degree of otherworldliness, such that one can understand why Nietzsche linked Plato with Christianity and saw both of them as life denying. But the problems found in Plato's flirtations with otherworldliness are not necessarily dealt with more adequately in Nietzsche's atheistic overreaction.

The locus of mystic philosophy in Plato's dialogues that most impresses Barnes is in the *Republic*, but not in the myth of the sun or the encounter with the form of the good. Rather, Barnes is interested in the Dantelike myth of Er, where the protagonist journeys to the dead and the about-to-be-born in order to report on what is really important in life. By ignoring the evidence in favor of Platonic belief in the World Soul, Barnes sees Plato as a pluralist, rather than as a cosmological monist. She is more insightful, I think, when she focuses on the extent to which Platonic mysticism forces us to learn how to live better here and now in *this* world, which is, to greater or lesser degrees, deified. The human soul can prepare the way for mystical deification by both *askesis*, on the model of athletic preparation for the "big event," and the life of the mind. Regarding the latter we should remember Whitehead's remark that the purpose of philosophy is to rationalize mysticism.[12]

BECOMING LIKE GOD

In two passages in the late dialogues (*Theaetetus* 176B–C and *Timaeus* 90A–D) we are encouraged to see the goal in human life as a becoming like the divine as far as possible (*homoiosis theoi kata to dynaton*). We have seen Plutarch claim that all of the ancient philosophers (excluding Aristotle and the atomists) saw God as the soul for the whole world, yet relatively few contemporary philosophers have even considered this as a possibility. So also in antiquity it was universally acknowledged, according to David Sedley, that the Platonic goal in life was to become as much like the divine as possible, yet today relatively few philosophers would see this as the primary goal in life.[13]

Assimilation to God obviously has moral consequences in terms of the supply of a divine standard for human justice, but equally important are the metaphysical or cosmological consequences that follow from an understanding of the fact that the World Soul and our own souls are remotely akin. It changes one's outlook quite a bit to come to believe that both the orderliness/beauty of the world as a whole and our own intellectual/aesthetic lives are the result of divine intelligence, as Sedley correctly argues. Further, assimilation to God, we learn in the *Timaeus* passage, is both intrinsically worthwhile and good for its primary effect of happiness (*eudaimonia*), reminding us of the fact that justice, too, in the second book of the *Republic* is viewed as valuable both in consummatory and in instrumental senses.

Assimilation to God is a return to the soul's "original" nature ("origin" here is not intended in a temporal way). Our end is in our beginning, as it were. To see assimilation to God as our *telos* means that such assimilation is both a goal aimed for and a supreme fulfillment. Assimilation to God as the World Soul is perhaps easier to understand when the World Soul is not seen as a detached intellect but as the governing (yet not omnipotent) intelligent force in the cosmos who is concerned with the good of the parts. The *homoiosis* is at once intellectual, aesthetic, moral, and metaphysical/cosmological.

Aristotle is to be thanked for his sometimes contradictory account of the relationship between the active life and the contemplative one because this comparison at least forces us to take the claims of each seriously. And he may be correct (see *Nicomachean Ethics* X, 7) in suggesting that it is the contemplative life that most directly assimilates us to God in that we demean God by saying that a divine being would need virtues such as courage and moderation, virtues that are crucial in the active life. Whom should God fear? How could God be tempted to be pleonexic? It must be admitted, according to Sedley, that Aristotle's status in Athens as a metic or as an alien, a status that seriously limited his rights, may have predisposed him toward the contemplative life. In any event, his ambivalent thoughts regarding the relative merits of the active and contemplative lives lead us to wonder whether Plato's *homoiosis* in effect moves us partially away from the gods of the polis and toward a cosmic religion, a point we have considered earlier in a treatment of Solmsen's interpretation of Plato.

In this regard we should consider seriously John Armstrong's claim that Plato's "becoming like God" involves far more than flight from the sensible world; it involves changing it for the better. This positive view of *homoiosis* is largely due to the conception of God as *nous* in the *Philebus*, *Timaeus*, and *Laws*, he thinks (although the *homoiosis* doctrine is found in the *Republic* as well—500C–D). In the *Philebus* we become like God because we are able to be intelligent causes of change; specifically, we can cause goodness to come about in the world. And regarding the *Laws* Armstrong insightfully notes the following:

> The *Laws*...helps to round out a picture of godlikeness begun in the *Philebus* and *Timaeus*. The guardians apply knowledge of the good to society by educating the citizens in virtue. Although most citizens do not approximate the divine as closely as the guardians, they can nonetheless make significant progress by subordinating their passions to the value judgments embodied in the city's laws. The one who cannot do this because of a lack of intelligence is said to be "bereft of god" ... (716A–B) while the one who obeys and whose soul is temperate is said to be "dear to god, for he is similar" (716C–D). Likeness to god is therefore a goal of all citizens, not just the guardians. For the guardians, though, the perfection of virtue demands not flight from the world but a fight to instill the order that intelligence prescribes.[14]

Some sort of rapprochement between the active life and the contemplative one is surely possible, as even Martha Nussbaum admits in her otherwise skeptical treatment of the Platonic preeminence of the contemplative life.[15] To take a contemporary example, Thomas Merton has clearly shown how even a cloistered monk can be politically engaged. And the Jesuits and the Quakers have historically provided many examples of how to be a contemplative-in-action. Plato himself offers us admonitions not only against too much concern for "this" world but also against a too aggressive asceticism, as in the defense of the mixed life in the *Philebus* (25D, 46A, 48B, 49A, 61C; also see *Laws* 792C–D), where the pleasures that follow upon the satisfaction of moderated appetites are necessary parts of the good life. Assimilation to God (seen as the World Soul) prevents us from becoming enslaved to any one part of the cosmos, even our own asceticism. The beauty of the World Soul enables us to see the (albeit lesser) beauty of ourselves.[16]

The effort to assimilate to God as far as possible proves futile, however, if God is seen as lifeless and unchanging. J. V. Luce concludes (mistakenly, I think) that Plato's flirtations in the dialogues with ontolatry constitute his entire theology.[17] Platonic mysticism involves personal contact between a human self-mover and a self-moving, an ever self-moving, cosmic soul.[18] As John Carmody notes, the striving to become as much like God as possible carries with it the satisfaction of being on the right, holy path, of doing the fully human thing. In this regard, religious believers in the Abrahamic religions do not need to "dehellenize" their faiths, as is sometimes alleged, but to "rehellenize" them along the lines of a more sophisticated Platonic philosophy of religion than the one that has been operative historically. Plato's cosmos *empsychos* is not a God who is *totaliter aliter*, as is the God of at least some Abrahamic believers. Strange as it sounds, Plato's World Soul, who is as close as breathing, can more easily be seen as a personal God than the strictly transcendent deity in some traditional Abrahamic theists who have been (wittingly or unwittingly) unduly influenced by Aristotle.[19]

Although not a process philosopher, the great philologist Ulrich von Wilamowitz-Moellendorff helps to counteract the tendency of many scholars, including Luce, to identify Plato's view of God in terms of static being. Wilamowitz thinks that *theos* in ancient Greece is primarily a predicative notion. The Greeks would not say that God is love or that God is an orderer but rather that love or orderliness are divine. This way of speaking is not entirely adequate for the purposes of contemporary philosophy of religion, but it does help in the effort to (ironically) trace a process or neoclassical view of God back to the classical period,[20] an effort that is crucial in trying to understand how one can assimilate as much as possible to God. One cannot assimilate to a changeless, lifeless abstraction. Perhaps even more helpful than Wilamowitz's view is Norman Pittinger's observation that the divine metaphysical attributes are best understood and used adverbially.[21] For example, "God exists wisely." In any event, both Wilamowitz and Pittinger insightfully help us to militate against description of God in terms of an unchanging substance.

In a second article on the *homoiosis theoi kata to dynaton*, Sedley rightly points out that Plato's stance here is influenced by the Pythagorean idea that the soul's progress points toward recovery of the "original" divinity from which it has fallen, a myth that shows structural similarities to that found in Genesis. Sedley is also correct to emphasize that Platonic assimilation to God is supposed to occur in our present lifespan. Confusion arises when passages such as those in *Symposium* (207C–09E) are considered, where procreation is the device whereby mortal creatures strive for a share of immortality, and hence of divinity, so far as possible (*kata to dynaton*). But if immortality is *the* mark of divinity, and *if* human beings are guaranteed immortality, then assimilation to God begins to look redundant. Luckily this theme recedes after the *Symposium*, on Sedley's insightful reading. The theme of striving after a divine paradigm remains, however.[22]

The context for the discussion of *homoiosis* in the *Theaetetus* fittingly involves the replacement of Protagorean relativism and localized values with cosmic, divine values (also see *Laws* 716C). These universal standards, as Sedley emphasizes, are not so much provided by the forms as by God. Presumably Sedley is implying a defense of the intradeical view of the forms discussed above in chapter 3. Quite ironically, we gain insight into the historical Socrates' view via the late dialogue *Theaetetus*: relativism can be resisted even without reference to the Platonic forms due to *religious* conviction. Both in the early dialogues and here in the later ones holiness (*hosiotes*) is a virtue, a fact that is sometimes missed by scholars who are overly familiar with the four cardinal virtues in the *Republic*. To be specific, holiness is the virtue connected to service of the divine, and since God is basically good, to serve God is the same thing as to lead a good life. That is, "the skill which enables us to serve god simply *is* the skill of being just, courageous, moderate, and wise."[23]

As before, I think that the main implication of the assimilation to God theme consists in a proper understanding of one's place in the cosmos, but Sedley is surely correct in also emphasizing the ethical implications of this theme. Variations on the *homoiosis* doctrine are found throughout Plato's dialogues in terms of the idea that happiness will come to the virtuous person as a divine gift: at the end of the *Apology* (41C–D), at the end of Diotima's speech in the *Symposium*, at the end of the *Republic* (613A–B), and so on. Sedley agrees, however, that in the *Theaetetus*, but especially in the *Timaeus*, the *homoiosis* doctrine is primarily cosmological or religious, rather than ethical: "The *Timaeus* is Plato's great attempt to show how the world can only be adequately understood if viewed as the product of divine intelligence. What emerges from it is that the human soul's capacity to pattern itself after a divine mind is far from accidental, but directly reflects the soul's own nature and origin and the teleological structure of the world as a whole."[24]

Becoming like God is, cosmologically speaking, the return of the rational part of the soul to its own "original" nature. We are, in effect, being asked to escape from any parochial perception and to view reality according to the thought patterns of the World Soul, who considers the good of the cosmos. Sedley sees the World Soul not only as divine but also as providential, albeit with limited power (due to metaphysical reasons detailed earlier in the book). Further, Sedley is one of the few commentators to notice that this requires us to think about becoming as well as being, presumably because the World Soul is not beyond the natural world of becoming but *is* that world conceived as an integral, besouled whole. I have reiterated the point throughout the present book that one need not interpret Plato as Aristotle did, to the effect that the cosmic God would adulterate the divine perfection by turning toward the changeable.[25]

In addition to Sedley's recent examination of the assimilation to God doctrine is that of Julia Annas, who variously sees the *homoiosis* passage in the *Theaetetus* as odd, outrageous, fantastic, a rhetorical overstatement, an embarrassment, a bafflement, and difficult to find sensible! These reactions, whether Annas' own or defended vicariously on the behalf of others, ultimately seem to be due to the fact that the Platonic view, wherein our final end is to become like God to the extent possible, just does not resonate with "us" in the contemporary world.[26] (To be frank, it resonates with me quite profoundly.) Even in a book titled *Platonic Piety* by Michael Morgan, she notes, the idea that becoming like God might be our *telos* is entirely ignored. The key difficulty seems to be that Annas and others assume that becoming like God necessarily involves an unworldliness or otherworldliness and an escape or flight from this world with its inevitable mixture of good with evil.

The whole point to the present book, however, is to hold that this assumption is incorrect, as Annas herself could have discovered on the evidence supplied in her own position. That is, at times she admits that her unsympathetic response to Plato's assimilation to God doctrine is mitigated by the possibility that one could fulfill all of one's civic duties yet still see some other matters as more important, as constitutive of one's real life.

On this interpretation, the assimilation to God doctrine is not a mere digression, as Annas sometimes indicates, nor does it entail an obliviousness to political struggles.[27] Rather, it is an acknowledgment that reason is our most divine part and that God just *is* reason or the divine in us. To be rational, however, we need to try, to the extent possible, to adopt the thought patterns of the universe, which Annas does not compare to certain features of Whitehead's or Hartshorne's philosophies, but surprisingly to the utilitarian Henry Sidgwick's impartial spectator view.

Annas is especially instructive in two ways. First, she notes that the request that we adopt the "point of view" of the *uni*verse is more conducive to (an implicit) monotheism than it is to the diverse divine points of view encouraged in polytheism. And second, she emphasizes the point that becoming like God is not so much a way to virtue and happiness, it just *is* virtue and happiness.[28] Implied here is the claim that God is omnibenevolent, even if a perfect being-in-becoming would perhaps have no need for virtues such as moderation or courage.

THEOCENTRISM

Evidence of a certain skepticism regarding what we can know and say about God appears regularly in Plato's dialogues (e.g., *Cratylus* 400D), but with divine help the situation is not hopeless (e.g., *Cratylus* 425C; *Republic* 492E). Plato's prime objection in this regard seems to be that some people are too confident in what they say about the gods on the evidence they receive from the encyclopedic Homeric poets and rhapsodes,[29] who produce the impression that it is easier to speak adequately about the gods than it is to do so about human beings such as ourselves (*Republic* 598E; *Critias* 107B). Plato, through the Athenian in the *Laws*, is willing to leave these stories about the gods to others (672B).

Two extremes are to be avoided, it seems: both the overconfidence of the Homeric poets and rhapsodes and the skepticism of the atheists, against whom are directed Plato's arguments for the existence of God. Human beings are capable of gradually working their way toward an adequate description of God, slow learners that we are (*Epinomis* 978E).

It should not escape our notice that if wisdom is found in God (a commonplace in Plato's dialogues), then there is something divine about the philosophic life, wherein one loves or searches for wisdom, either through dialectical exchange with others or through thinking, where one in effect dialogues with oneself (*Sophist* 216B, 254A–B; *Statesman* 285B).

An appreciation of Plato's theocentrism is enhanced through an appeal to passages throughout the dialogues, from early to late, that indicate a familiarity with religious experience. For example, Socrates in the *Apology* (e.g., 40B) is famous for the divine sign or voice that he had received, but in the *Phaedo* (60E) he is visited by the divine through dreams. On these bases we should not be surprised to learn of the importance of contemplation in Socrates' life (*Phaedo* 84A, 111B).

Further, the character Socrates is divinely inspired in the middle dialogues as well as in the early ones (*theion pathos peponthenai*—*Phaedrus* 238C); indeed he admits that he possesses a divining power (*Phaedrus* 242B–D; 244A–45C). This should not be interpreted as a glorified humanity or apotheosis, as I have used this term above, but rather as a condition in which one is possessed by deity (*Phaedrus* 249D, 250B). Likewise, in the *Symposium* (e.g., 175B–C) there are the character Socrates' famous trances, which are presumably divinely inspired. Contemplation of the divine is also found in the *Republic* (517D) on the well-known way of ascent (521C, 526E).

Obviously I have only scratched the surface of the topic of religious experience in Plato's early and middle dialogues, but enough passages have been cited to set the stage for a consideration of how this topic is treated in the late dialogues, which are my primary concern.

Although the character Socrates in the *Theaetetus* indicates that his midwife's art, wherein he enables others to learn the truth, is a divine gift (210C), it is also clear that this Socrates himself is not permitted to suppress the truth (151A, 151D). Of course it is one thing to say that one has a duty not to suppress the truth and another to ascertain exactly what the truth is (see *Timaeus* 71–72). Through the divine gift of education, however, the task is not impossible (*Laws* 653C–54A). Clinias in the *Laws* (968C) even asks us to take seriously belief in divine providence, such that it is God who guides us along the road of life. The Athenian in the *Epinomis* (presumably Plato) makes virtually the same point (980C). For the purposes of this chapter it should be noted that at times this divine guidance reaches us in a flash of understanding when we are flooded with light, as Plato attests regarding (presumably?) his own personal experience (*Seventh Letter* 344B).

Consider once again the crucial theocentric passage in the *Theaetetus* (176A–C), where we are encouraged to become as much like the divine as possible. At the very least this means that we must, through the self-motions of our own souls along with divine guidance, do more than just seem good; we must be such. And being good, in contrast to seeming so, requires a life of reason and intelligence (*noein kai phronein*—*Philebus* 33B). At both

Theaetetus (176A–C) and *Timaeus* (90A–D), the two most significant passages in the dialogues regarding theocentrism, we find that intellect just *is* the spark of divinity in human beings; it is that part of human beings whereby they can, to the extent that it is possible, assimilate to divinity.

That is, in contrast to Protagoras' anthropocentric dictum that "man is the measure of all things," we have in Plato the theocentric claim that such a measure is in God (*Laws* 716C–D). When compared to such a sublime standard, human beings might very well think that there is something ludic or playful about their own lives, but we need not be discouraged by this prospect in that we can still make our play as perfect as possible (see *Laws* 803C; also see 774A, 801A–E). However, this is only one possibility. Most religious believers take their lives quite seriously. A necessary step toward wisdom is taken when we realize that the seriousness of our lives only makes sense when we see them as contributions to the World Soul, rather than the other way around. This does not necessarily mean that we have to sacrifice our individual happinesses for the sake of the whole in that perhaps the most significant contribution that each of us can make to the whole is the individual happiness that is partially within our control. By virtue of the common "origin" in soul, what is best for the whole is also best for us as individuals. This is the whole point to *homoiosis* (see *Laws* 903C–D; also see 809D, 821A–B, 899D, 966C; finally see *Epinomis* 989B–C). As Brian Henning aptly puts the point, an individual's value is all three at once: value for itself, value for others, and value for the whole.

One of the problems involved in contemporary scholars coming to terms with mysticism in Plato is that the designation *mystic* is used to refer to two theoretically distinct persons: (1) the one who has had immediate experience of God or (2) the one who insists that God is ineffable or who says that God can only be characterized in paradoxical, or, at least seemingly, contradictory ways.[30] The two designations seem quite distinct in that we can imagine them predicated of individuals separately, even if some individual mystics are deserving of being called "mystics" in both senses of the term. However, it is the first sense that seems to be primary in Plato's dialogues because ineffability has a carefully demarcated role to play in his thought, as we have seen. That is, Plato has the characters in his dialogues say a great deal about the "ineffable."

Concerning the first sense of the term *mystic*, Hartshorne has made some important observations. It would be odd, he thinks, if a ubiquitous being-in-becoming could only be known or affirmed indirectly. But if direct contact with God requires true solitude (see the *Seventh Letter*, where Plato indicates the need to escape from the dizzying swirl of current events and political intrigue), we can understand why many would think that no direct contact with God is possible. Regarding the rarity of true solitude, Hartshorne says the following: "Infants and subhuman animals do little introspecting, and the rest of us are more like them in this than we usually admit."[31] If solitude occurs, however, one in solitude can learn that the most readily detectable data are those that are sometimes present, sometimes not, like redness or pain. What is always given tends to escape notice. Consider the claim, made by many, not to experience spatial extension in sounds (although they experience it in colors), despite the fact that spatiality is given in all experiences, even auditory or religious ones. Or consider the fact that human feeling is largely "feeling of feeling," in that we can feel as individuals only because our cells (or, for the Greeks, nerves) can feel at a primitive level. In localized pain we become aware of what we could always be aware of: we are composed of tiny, albeit living, loci of feeling whose cell walls can be damaged and agitated.

Now we can know that the extended cosmos is a society of sentient creatures whose influences upon one another conform largely to the patterns traced by physics. Theists influenced by Plato are likely to call this society "God" or the "World Soul," a personal being who imposes limits upon mutual conflict and disorder in the natural world. That is, the pervasive unity of the world is, somehow, an aspect of divine unity. As Hartshorne puts the matter: "the difference between mystics and others [is] a relative, not an absolute one. The mystic is one who is aware of experiencing what we all do experience, whether aware of the fact or not. In mystics unconscious intuition, in the sense in which infants and the lower animals are unconscious, that is, without introspective judgments, becomes also conscious."[32]

The key to appreciating a Platonic philosophy of religion of the sort defended in the present book is to get beyond the simplistic alternative between either a traditional, omnipotent God who coercively moves the world or a world that is cosmologically directionless. If reality is, by its very nature, relational (i.e., if being *is* dynamic power to affect, or to be affected by, others), then we should not so much say that it is the world that sets the limits to divine power but that it is the divine nature itself that does so.[33] This is due to the fact that the greatest conceivable being would be the most relative of all in the sense that God is not related merely to some others, with their own dynamic powers, but to all of them.

The language of Whitehead may help here. Most human beings "prehend" God in the sense that they grasp implicitly meaning in the world. That is, they feel as an inchoate object of experience that they are parts of a meaningful whole, that there is a concrete fact of relatedness between themselves and a personal force at work in the cosmos, the World Soul. But the subjective form this prehension takes in the mystic is that of an explicit, conscious "apprehension." In effect, the prehension/apprehension distinction is analogous to the Leibnizian distinction between perception/apperception, with the mystic exhibiting an acuity with respect to the latter element in these pairs that the rest of us possess only potentially. This acuity, however, is not aggressive, as the Platonist Wordsworth (who, along with Plato himself and Leibniz, influenced Whitehead and Hartshorne) noticed: "I deem that there are Powers/Which of themselves our minds impress;/That we can feed this mind of ours/In a wise passiveness." We fail to feed our minds this wise passiveness largely because "The world is too much with us; late and soon,/Getting and spending, we lay waste our powers."[34]

However, to say that "the world is too much with us" is not necessarily to say that we should try to escape from it. Rather, the point seems to be that in a Platonic philosophy of religion we need to alter our approach to the world in that God is our savior (sotera—once again, see Timaeus 48D) by giving us intellect and the ability to do philosophy. Platonic redemption, if it is not too misleading to use this word, obviously does not consist in a guarantee of the entire elimination of evil. This is impossible due to the self-motion of besouled creatures, the contrast/collision among such self-motions, and the fading of value in a world of becoming. Platonic faith in the face of evil is expressed best in the famous lines from Wordsworth:

> Though nothing can bring back the hour
> Of splendour in the grass, of glory in the flower;
> We will grieve not, rather find
> Strength in what remains behind;
> In the primal sympathy
> Which having been must ever be;
> In the soothing thoughts that spring
> Out of human suffering;
> In the faith that looks through death,
> In years that bring the philosophic mind.[35]

In the midst of evil there is the ontological priority of an all-good God, seen as the preeminent Self-Mover, who is both the ground of novelty and the preserver of value in a universe in flux. That is, on a Platonic basis "redemption" consists not in an absence of evil, in that it is impossible to have higher forms of psyche without having an increased sensitivity to pain; by way of contrast, the lilies of the field neither toil nor suffer.[36]

To completely eliminate evil would be to eliminate the self-motion and temporality that make our lives possible. We are "redeemed" by God *in* this world and not *from* it. On this view the ultimate evil is not death, as Plato himself realized, but the loss of the sense of the value and point to our lives. Although we suffer, these sufferings are taken up into the merciful (*eleountas*—once again, see *Laws* 665A) World Soul and are transformed by becoming parts of a magnificent whole. It is precisely this magnificent whole that the mystic receives back, including its transfigured sufferings.

IMITATING GOD

For the purposes of the present book it is important to emphasize the connection between the imitation of God doctrine, on the one hand, and the dipolar, process nature of God in Plato's dialogues, on the other. Culbert Rutenber is a classicist who is very instructive regarding this connection, such that an examination of his view will be helpful in the effort to summarize the major contributions of the present book.

Imitation of the divine is intimated in the *Republic* (613), but this doctrine can be found more explicitly in Plato's late dialogues in terms of both the language of *homoiosis theoi*, when humans consciously imitate God, and *paraplesia heautoi*, when the rest of the cosmos unconsciously does so. Words related to the imitation in question include *mimesis*, obviously, but also the Greek word for participation (*methexis*). Rutenber is one of the few commentators to emphasize that in the *Sophist* (248E) we learn that perfection implies not only mind but also life and soul. Hence in imitating God one imitates not only the greatest mind but also the most dynamic: a *living*, besouled, and most good reality. Indeed, mind can only exist within a living soul (*Philebus* 30C; *Sophist* 249A; *Timaeus* 30B, 37C, 46D; and *Laws* 961D).[37]

The view of God as simply immutable rests on the assumption, made by many scholars, that God is to be identified with the immutable form of the good.[38] But we have seen that the steadfastness of divine goodness, implied in God's everlasting knowledge of the form of the good, is nonetheless compatible with God's providential interest in the world of change. Plato is presumably influenced in his view of God both by philosophic argument and by religious experience of a personal God, even if the Greeks, as Rutenber notices, did not have a word that corresponded exactly to our word *person*. Wilamowitz, however, focuses on the personal*izing* process involved in Platonic theism in that God is decidedly not an empty abstraction if God is a self-moving soul (a redundancy, perhaps).[39]

Plato's God is a soul, not a form, not even the form of the good.[40] Further, Plato's God is *a* soul or *the* God, indicating a strong tendency toward monotheism in his thought (see *Phaedo* 106D; *Republic* 382D, 597C; and *Laws* 913D), even if Plato sometimes uses the singular as well as the plural for deity in the same passage. This one besouled deity (the World Soul) just is the omniscient mind imaginatively symbolized by the Demiurge in the *Timaeus*, on Rutenber's insightful reading.[41] The text indicates not only that Platonic philosophers desire to imitate God but also that the Demiurge desires that philosophers should be as much like the divine as possible (29E). Human assimilation to God (*homoiosis*) and nonhuman likeness to God (*paraplesia*) indicate that the imitation of God doctrine in the late dialogues continues the tendency found in the middle dialogues to encourage participation (*methexis*) in the forms, at least when these are seen as the contents of divine thoughts. And there is some evidence of the imitation of God doctrine itself even in the middle dialogues (e.g., *Phaedrus* 252D).

Although Plato's forms are presumably changeless, the effort of each particular to fulfill the possibilities of its type (i.e., the effort to achieve its *arete*) involves considerable movement. In spite of the human failures to achieve *arete*, God continues to shepherd the world (or better, to weave together the self-motions in the cosmos—see the *Statesman* 269 ff.), according to Plato's theory of motion (*kinesis*) that emerges in the late dialogues. We should not fail to notice that thinking itself is a kind of motion in Plato (*Timaeus* 47B; *Laws* 897D). So is love, as is detailed in the more famous passages in the *Symposium* and *Phaedrus*. And the human mind is akin to the divine mind (*Philebus* 30A; *Timaeus* 41C, 47B). One of the key consequences of the present book's Platonic defense of divine omniscience and rejection of divine omnipotence is that the divine intellect is seen as more ultimate than divine power. I assume that something like this is implied in the *Euthyphro* (10Dff.) when it is claimed that the divine loves the holy just because it *is* holy and not because an omnipotent God makes it so.

If God is a soul, and if soul is defined in terms of self-motion, then God in some way must "participate in" (or better, and more simply, "know") the form of motion. The dynamism of God, along with the frequent evidence in favor of God's omnibenevolence (*Philebus* 22C; *Theaetetus* 176A–B; *Timaeus* 29E, etc.), lead to what is, in effect, the ensoulment of the good or the highest possible moving good, as Rutenber rightly urges.[42] If God knows ideally the form of the good, then imitating the form of the good and imitating God are very close to being the same thing, even if they are not identical. In imitating God one is not imitating an all-powerful being who has hegemony over recalcitrant necessity (*anangke*). Nonetheless, even the brute facts of the world "imitate" God in the sense that they are brought in some fashion into an orderly cosmos to the extent that this is possible in a universe pervaded by at least partial self-motion. Even an "irrational" number, like the square root of two, can be cajoled into a system of mathematics that is, as a whole, quite rational. The fact that the cosmos is indissoluble indicates the extent of God's rational power, if not of God's omnipotence.

It might be objected that it is impossible for us to become like God because we are embodied, whereas God is not. But Plato's cosmological monism, indeed his cosmological hylomorphism, is such that the World Soul and the body of the world go together. Once Plato's gods and daemons are seen as analogous to the saints in Catholic tradition, in that the religion of the masses tends to be emotional and symbolic rather than intellectual,[43] the cogency of the claim that Plato is a cosmological monist or a cosmological hylomorphist can be seen more easily. Like the strength of a magnet (*Ion* 533D–E), God attracts both us and other parts of the cosmos, although the attraction grows increasingly faint as we reach the most insignificant parts of the whole.

Rutenber shows a vague awareness of the similarity between his own view of Plato and Whitehead's view of Plato. But he exhibits confusion regarding exactly how to reconcile the dynamic elements of Plato's theism with the fact that there is something immutable that is praised by Plato. As I see things, this confusion is typical of commentators who have not taken seriously enough the process approach to Plato. It is my hope that the chapter "Dipolar Theism" is helpful in this regard: the fact that God always exists and is always all-good is indeed not subject to change, but how God exists or the mode of God's existence (i.e., God's actuality rather than God's existence) is constantly changing.

Rutenber is on stronger grounds when he emphasizes the fact that the one who is most just (*dikaistatas*) is the one who is most like God (*Republic* 613Aff.; *Theaetetus* 176C). That is, there need be no conflict between imitation of God and the civic virtues if the God who is imitated is most wise. In this regard we should take note of the fact that there is no distinction in Plato, as there is in Aristotle, between *sophia* (theoretical wisdom) and *phronesis* (practical wisdom—*Republic* 428B; *Phaedo* 79D; *Meno* 88C–89A). Someone who assimilates to God and nonetheless performs civic virtue is not necessarily like a hermit who is called to the papal chair, as Ernest Barker seems to allege. Meditation on the divine is not opposed to action; it is the spring from which all significant effort derives, as Rutenber perceptively notes.[44]

By working for the best—in religion, politics, art, education, and so on—we imitate God, who exhibits the virtue not only of wisdom but also, in peculiar ways, the virtues of moderation and courage. Divine moderation consists not in confrontation with temptation, but in a state of graciousness or equanimity (*ileon*—*Laws* 792C–D). Likewise, divine courage consists not in a confrontation with fear, but in a resolute fight to maintain and increase goodness (*Laws* 900D, 901E). It is easy to see why this God cannot be bribed through petitionary prayer; on a Platonic basis prayer consists in an aspiration to adjust one's inner attitude to cosmic, divine harmony (*Phaedrus* 279B; *Laws* 664B–C). The goal of assimilation to God *to the extent possible* (*kata to dynaton*) involves the contrast between our imperfect and intermittent vision of the forms and God's perfect and unwavering vision. Our vision is intermittent in part because of the clamor of our distractions. The point to Platonic *askesis* is to enable us to be less distracted away from what is really important in life.

Notes

NOTES TO THE INTRODUCTION

1. Alfred North Whitehead, *Process and Reality*, corrected edition (New York: Free Press, 1978), p. 39; also see p. 7.

2. On Whitehead's "footnotes" quotation, see Richard Kraut, "Introduction to the Study of Plato," in Richard Kraut, ed., *The Cambridge Companion to Plato* (Cambridge: Cambridge University Press, 1992), p. 32.

3. Nicholas Smith, "Platonic Scholars and Other Wishful Thinkers," in James Klagge and Nicholas Smith, eds., *Methods of Interpreting Plato and His Dialogues* (Oxford: Clarendon, 1992), pp. 245–59.

4. Ibid., pp. 251, 255.

5. See Hartshorne's quotation in Randall Auxier and Mark Davies, eds., *Hartshorne and Brightman on God, Process, and Persons: The Correspondence, 1922–1945* (Nashville: Vanderbilt University Press, 2001), p. 62.

6. See Giovanni Reale, *Toward a New Interpretation of Plato* (Washington, DC: Catholic University of America Press, 1997), pp. xxi–xxiii.

7. See Walter Burkert, *Greek Religion* (Cambridge: Harvard University Press, 1985), p. 322.

8. Ibid., p. 325.

9. Ibid., p. 328.

10. See Joseph Brennan's summary of Whitehead's course at Harvard on cosmology, "Whitehead on Plato's Cosmology," *Journal of the History of Philosophy* 9 (1971), p. 70.

11. Ibid., pp. 73, 76.

12. Robert O'Connell, "God, Gods, and Moral Cosmos in Socrates' Apology," *International Philosophical Quarterly* 25 (1985), p. 31.

13. G. M. A. Grube, *Plato's Thought* (London: Methuen, 1935), p. 151.

14. Hartshorne relies here on Julius Stenzel, *Plato's Method of Dialectic* (Oxford: Clarendon, 1940).

15. Here Hartshorne cites Schleiermacher's view of Plato and the work of Raphael Demos, *The Philosophy of Plato* (New York: Scribner's, 1939).

16. See Charles Hartshorne, *Philosophers Speak of God* (Chicago: University of Chicago Press, 1953), pp. 38–39.

17. It should be noted, however, that in Hartshorne's private library, now archived at the Center for Process Studies at the Claremont Graduate School, can be found several marked copies of various Plato dialogues, as well as several secondary studies on Plato, including Ronald Levinson, *In Defense of Plato* (Cambridge: Harvard University Press, 1953).

18. See Charles Hartshorne, *Philosophers Speak of God*, p. 40. Also see William Prior, *Unity and Development in Plato's Metaphysics* (LaSalle, IL: Open Court, 1985); as the title indicates, unity and development in Plato's metaphysics are not contradictory.

19. See Randall Auxier and Mark Davies, eds., *Hartshorne and Brightman on God, Process, and Persons: The Correspondence, 1922–1945*, pp. 93–94.

20. Leonard Brandwood, *The Chronology of Plato's Dialogues* (Cambridge: Cambridge University Press, 1990). In addition to Brandwood, see several other scholars on the longstanding belief that there are stages in Plato's career: Robert Turnbull, *The "Parmenides" and Plato's Late Philosophy* (Toronto: University of Toronto Press, 1998); John Rist, "The Order of the Later Dialogues of Plato," *Phoenix* 14 (1960), pp. 207–21; and T. M. Robinson, "The Relative Dating of the *Timaeus* and *Phaedrus*," in Livio Rossetti, ed., *Understanding the "Phaedrus"* (Sankt Augustin, Germany: Academia Verlag, 1992), pp. 23–30.

21. For example, consider the skepticism of Jacob Howland, "Re-Reading Plato: The Problem of Platonic Chronology," *Phoenix* 45 (1991), pp. 189–214; and Holger Thesleff, "Platonic Chronology," *Phoenix* 34 (1989), pp. 1–26.

22. See the last chapter of my *Divine Beauty: The Aesthetics of Charles Hartshorne* (Nashville: Vanderbilt University Press, 2004).

23. See James Beckman, *The Religious Dimension of Socrates' Thought* (Waterloo, Canada: Wilfried Laurier University Press, 1979); Mark McPherran, *The Religion of Socrates* (University Park: Penn State University Press, 1999); Nicholas Smith and Paul Woodruff, eds., *Reason and Religion in Socratic Philosophy* (Oxford: Oxford University Press, 2000); and Hans-Georg Gadamer, "Religion and Religiosity in Socrates," *Proceedings of the Boston Area Colloquium in Ancient Philosophy* 1 (1985), pp. 53–76.

24. See two helpful anthologies: Charles Griswold, ed., *Platonic Writings, Platonic Readings* (New York: Routledge, 1988); and Gerald Press, ed., *Who Speaks for Plato?* (Lanham, MD; Rowman and Littlefield, 2000).

25.   See Kenneth Sayre, "Why Plato Never Had a Theory of Forms," *Proceedings of the Boston Area Colloquium in Ancient Philosophy* 9 (1993), pp. 167–99. Cf., Charles Griswold, "Commentary on Sayre's 'Why Plato Never Had a Theory of Forms,'" *Proceedings of the Boston Area Colloquium in Ancient Philosophy* 9 (1993), pp. 200–12, who throws the baby out with the bathwater by saying that not only did Plato not have a theory of forms, but he did not have a theory regarding *any* important topic.

26.   Kenneth Sayre, *Plato's Literary Garden: How to Read a Platonic Dialogue* (Notre Dame: University of Notre Dame Press, 1995).

27.   Patricia Cook, "Neville's Use of Plato," in J. H. Chapman, ed., *Interpreting Neville* (Albany: State University of New York Press, 1999), pp. 45–57.

28.   See Charles Griswold, "*E Pluribus Unum?* On the Platonic 'Corpus,'" *Ancient Philosophy* 19 (1999), pp. 361–97; and Charles Kahn, "Response to Griswold," *Ancient Philosophy* 20 (2000), pp. 189–93.

29.   Richard Kraut, "Introduction to the Study of Plato," p. 25.

30.   See James Collins, *The Emergence of Philosophy of Religion* (New Haven: Yale University Press, 1967). Also see Gerard Naddaf, "Plato's *Theologia* Revisited," *Methexis* 9 (1996), pp. 5–18, where the author attempts to clear up a controversy involving Gregory Vlastos and others regarding the concept of 'theology' in Plato: the "science" of things divine.

31.   William Lane Craig, *The Cosmological Argument from Plato to Leibniz* (New York: Barnes and Noble, 1980), p. 11.

32.   See the following studies: C. W. P. Pehrson, "Plato's Gods," *Polis* 9 (1990), pp. 122–69; Kathryn Morgan, *Myth and Philosophy from the Pre-Socratics to Plato* (Cambridge: Cambridge University Press, 2000); Markus Enders, "Platons 'Theologie': Der Gott, die Gotter und das Gute," *Perspektiven-der-Philosophie* 25 (1999), pp. 131–85; Frederick Sontag, "The Faces of God," *Man and World* 8 (1975), pp. 70–81; and Gerd Van Riel, *Plato's Gods* (Burlington, VT: Ashgate, forthcoming).

33.   Roy Wood Sellars' way of stating the intradeical, rather than extradeical, interpretation of Plato is to say that forms or eternal objects are tinged with the quality of feeling. See Sellars' "Philosophy of Organism and Physical Realism," in P. A. Schilpp, ed., *The Philosophy of Alfred North Whitehead* (LaSalle, IL: Open Court, 1971), pp. 407–33.

Notes to Chapter One

1.   See Charles Hartshorne, *The Zero Fallacy and Other Essays in Neoclassical Metaphysics* (LaSalle, IL: Open Court, 1997), pp. 15, 32, 34, 58; also see pp. 75–76, 88–90, 96–97.

2.   Ibid., pp. 71–72.

3.   Richard Mohr, *The Platonic Cosmology* (Leiden: Brill, 1985), p. 175. See pp. 171–77 on the World Soul; pp. 178–83 on soul; pp. 53–84 on time and eternity; pp. 85–98 on flux and space; and pp. 158–70, 184–88 on theodicy.

4.   Ibid., pp. 171–77. Whereas the Demiurge is found primarily in the *Timaeus*, it is also implied in the *Phaedo* (97C–D) in terms of universal intelligence. Also see Gretchen Reydams-Schils, "Plato's World Soul," in Tomas Calvo and Luc Brisson, eds., *Interpreting the "Timaeus-Critias"* (Sankt Augustin, Germany: Academia Verlag, 1997), pp. 261–65, who sees the World Soul's function as essentially cognitive. Also see Richard Mohr's "Plato's Theology Reconsidered: What the Demiurge Does," *History of Philosophy Quarterly* 2 (1985), pp. 131–44.

5.   I deal with Swinburne in detail in "Does God Have a Body?" *The Journal of Speculative Philosophy* 2 (1988), pp. 225–32. For a phenomenological treatment of the world as a personal cosmos see Erazim Kohak, *The Embers and the Stars* (Chicago: University of Chicago Press, 1984).

6.   Richard Mohr, *The Platonic Cosmology*, p. 40.

7.   Plato sometimes refers to the World Soul by popular names such as *Uranus* or *Cosmos*. See *Epinomis* 977A–B, 978C, 987B. Also see Anne Ashbaugh, *Plato's Theory of Explanation: A Study of the Cosmological Account in the Timaeus* (Albany: State University of New York Press, 1988).

8.   See Friedrich Solmsen, "Greek Philosophy and the Discovery of Nerves," *Museum Helveticum* 18 (1961), pp. 150–67, 169–97.

9.   See Charles Hartshorne, *Man's Vision of God* (New York: Harper's, 1941), p. 153.

10.   See Charles Hartshorne, *Insights and Oversights of Great Thinkers* (Albany: State University of New York Press, 1983), pp. 30, 366. Also see Edgar Brightman, "Platonism," in Vergilius Ferm, ed., *An Encyclopedia of Religion* (New York: Philosophical Library, 1945); Hartshorne thinks that Brightman fails to appreciate the religious significance of Plato's notion of soul, including the World Soul.

11.   See Charles Hartshorne, *Creative Synthesis and Philosophic Method* (LaSalle, IL: Open Court, 1970), p. 116.

12.   See Charles Hartshorne, *Anselm's Discovery* (LaSalle, IL: Open Court, 1965), p. 293.

13.   See Charles Hartshorne, *Creativity in American Philosophy* (Albany: State University of New York Press, 1984), pp. 203, 251, 274.

14.   Charles Hartshorne, *Man's Vision of God*, p. 180.

15.   See Charles Hartshorne, *Whitehead's Philosophy* (Lincoln: University of Nebraska Press, 1972), pp. 53–54. Also see note 8 above.

16.   See Charles Hartshorne, *Reality as Social Process* (Boston: Beacon, 1953), pp. 138, 190.

17.   See Charles Hartshorne, *A Natural Theology for Our Time* (LaSalle, IL: Open Court, 1967), pp. 21, 99.

18.   See Charles Hartshorne, *Omnipotence and Other Theological Mistakes* (Albany: State University of New York Press, 1984), pp. 52–53, 59, 94. Also see Robert Turnbull, *The "Parmenides" and Plato's Late Philosophy*, pp. 142, 149, 165–66, 186, where the author at several points refers to "the mind of the World Animal," which I assume is the Demiurge.

19.   Charles Hartshorne, *Omnipotence and Other Theological Mistakes*, pp. 133–35. Also see Hartshorne, *Insights and Oversights of Great Thinkers*, p. 348. Finally, see Randall Auxier and Mark Davies, eds., *Hartshorne and Brightman on God, Process, and Persons: The Correspondence, 1922–1945*, pp. 66–69.

20.   Friedrich Solmsen, *Plato's Theology* (Ithaca: Cornell University Press, 1942), p. 8. Also see T. M. Robinson, "Understanding the *Timaeus*," *Proceedings of the Boston Area Colloquium in Ancient Philosophy* 2 (1986), pp. 103–19; and Donald Zeyl, "Commentary on 'Understanding the *Timaeus*,'" *Proceedings of the Boston Area Colloquium in Ancient Philosophy* 2 (1986), pp. 120–25.

21.   Friedrich Solmsen, *Plato's Theology*, pp. 40, 43, 46, 50–51, and 92. Also see F. M. Cornford, *Greek Religious Thought* (London: Dent, 1923); R. K. Hack, *God in Greek Philosophy to the Time of Socrates* (Princeton: Princeton University Press, 1931); and Pierre Bovet, *Le Dieu de Platon d'apres l'ordre chronologique des dialogues* (Geneve: Kundig, 1902). To use Aristotelian language, the forms supply the formal cause, and the Demiurge, the efficient cause in the creation of an orderly world; see Erik Ostenfeld, "The Role and Status of the Forms in the *Timaeus*," in Thomas Calvo and Luc Brisson, eds., *Interpreting the "Timaeus-Critias"*, pp. 167–77.

22.   See Jonathan Barnes, *The Presocratic Philosophers* (London: Routledge and Kegan Paul, 1979), p. 196; J. M. Robinson, *An Introduction to Early Greek Philosophy* (New York: Houghton Mifflin, 1968), p. 77; John Burnet, *Early Greek Philosophy* (London: Black, 1930), pp. 49, 75; and Charles Kahn, *The Art and Thought of Heraclitus* (Cambridge: Cambridge University Press, 1981), pp. 11, 171, 208, 268, 275, 278, and 337.

23.   See William Goodwin, ed., *Plutarch's Morals* (Boston: Little, Brown 1870), vol. 3, p. 133, "Whether the World Be an Animal."

24.   See Friedrich Solmsen, *Plato's Theology*, pp. 63–64, 68–69, 72–73.

25.   See F. M. Cornford, *Plato's Timaeus* (Indianapolis: Bobbs-Merrill, 1959), p. 28. Also see Brian Eucalano, "The Universal Soul," *Dialogue* 21 (1978), pp. 25–30; Conrad Bonifazi, *The Soul of the World: An Account of the Inwardness of Things* (Washington, DC: University Press of America, 1978); and Robert Whittemore, "The Proper Categorization of Plato's Demiurgos," *Tulane Studies in Philosophy* 27 (1978), pp. 163–66, who emphasizes Plato's panentheism.

26. For two good summaries of the doctrine of the World Soul in the *Timaeus* see W. K. C. Guthrie, *A History of Greek Philosophy* (Cambridge: Cambridge University Press, 1978), vol. 5, pp. 292–99; and Paul Shorey, *What Plato Said* (Chicago: University of Chicago Press, 1933), pp. 332–35.

27. See Friedrich Solmsen, *Plato's Theology*, pp. 77–80, 84–85.

28. See J. N. Findlay, *Plato: The Written and Unwritten Doctrines* (New York: Humanities, 1974), pp. 280–81, 297, 304, 311–14. Also see Findlay, "The Three Hypostases of Platonism," *Review of Metaphysics* 28 (1975), pp. 660–80.

29. J. N. Findlay, *Plato: The Written and Unwritten Doctrines*, p. 375. Also see Charles Hartshorne's *Omnipotence and Other Theological Mistakes*, p. 15; *Insights and Oversights of Great Thinkers*, p. 16; and *Creative Synthesis and Philosophic Method*, p. 121. Other relevant material from Hartshorne can be found in *Philosophers Speak of God*, pp. 211–12, 221. Finally, see Robert Whittemore, "Panentheism in Neo-Platonism," *Tulane Studies in Philosophy* 15 (1966), pp. 47–70; Joseph Moreau, *L'Ame du monde de Platon aux Stoiciens* (Paris: Societe d'edition Les Belles Lettres, 1939), pp. 75 ff.; and my own "An Anticipation of Hartshorne: Plotinus on *Daktylos* and the World Soul," *The Heythrop Journal* 29 (1988), pp. 462–67.

30. See Friedrich Solmsen, *Plato's Theology*, pp. 89–94, 98, 102, 107.

31. See P. E. More, *The Religion of Plato* (Princeton: Princeton University Press, 1921), pp. 89, 113, 116–17, 172, 223. Also see Gregory Vlastos, *Plato's Universe* (Seattle: University of Washington Press, 1975), pp. 25–27, 29, 31.

32. See Friedrich Solmsen, *Plato's Theology*, pp. 112–17.

33. Ibid., pp. 125–26.

34. See Paul Friedlander, *Plato* (New York: Pantheon, 1958), vol. 1, p. 31; and vol. 3, pp. 328, 348, 363, 365, 436.

35. See Hans-Georg Gadamer, *Dialogue and Dialectic* (New Haven: Yale University Press, 1980), pp. 140–46, 164–67. Also see Friedrich Solmsen, *Plato's Theology*, pp. 132–34, 138–40, 147.

36. See Friedrich Solmsen, *Plato's Theology*, pp. 152–54, 156.

37. See Jurgen Moltmann, *God in Creation* (San Francisco: Harper and Row, 1985).

38. See Friedrich Solmsen, *Plato's Theology*, pp. 162, 168–69.

39. See A. E. Taylor, *A Commentary on Plato's Timaeus* (Oxford: Clarendon, 1928), especially pp. 77–78, 80, 82, 103, 105, 124, 255–56. Also see Richard Patterson, "The Unique Worlds of the *Timaeus*," *Phoenix* 35 (1981), pp. 105–19.

40. See Friedrich Solmsen, *Plato's Theology*, p. 172. Also see Mary Gill, "Matter and Flux in Plato's *Timaeus*," *Phronesis* 32 (1987), pp. 34–53. Finally,

see Alois Rust, *Die Organismische Kosmologie von Alfred N. Whitehead* (Frankfurt: Athenaum, 1987) on Whitehead's debt to Plato.

41. See Origen, *On First Principles* (Gloucester, MA: Smith, 1973), especially 17.II.1.3. An article of mine largely deals with Origen, "Nature as Personal," *Philosophy and Theology* 5 (1990), pp. 81–96. Also see Friedrich Solmsen, *Plato's Theology*, pp. 177–95.

42. See Charles Hartshorne, *Insights and Oversights of Great Thinkers*, pp. x–xi; and *Creative Synthesis and Philosophic Method*, pp. 22, 159.

43. Friedrich Solmsen, *Plato's Theology*, p. 170.

44. See Charles Hartshorne, *Hartshorne and Brightman on God, Process, and Persons: The Correspondence, 1922–1945*, pp. 66–69. Cf. Ernst Mayr, who thinks that Plato's view of the cosmos as a living animal had a negative effect on biology; see "A Response to David Kitt's 'Plato on Kinds of Animals,'" *Biology and Philosophy* 3 (1988), pp. 592–96.

45. See Alfred North Whitehead, *Process and Reality*, pp. xiv, 94–96.

46. See Richard Parry, "The Intelligible World-Animal in Plato's *Timaeus*," *Journal of the History of Philosophy* 29 (1991), pp. 13–32. Also see Duane Voskuil, "Hartshorne, God, and Metaphysics: How the Cosmically Inclusive Personal Nexus and the World Interact," *Process Studies* 28 (1999), pp. 212–28.

NOTES TO CHAPTER TWO

1. See, e.g., Willem De Vries, "On *Sophist* 255B-E," *History of Philosophy Quarterly* 5 (1988), pp. 385–94. James Duerlinger, "The Ontology of Plato's *Sophist*," *Modern Schoolman* 65 (1988), pp. 151–84, also points out the metaphysical limitations of linguistic analysis in the examination of Plato's later dialogues. Also see Jean Roberts, "The Problem about Being in the *Sophist*," *History of Philosophy Quarterly* 3 (1986), pp. 229–43. Finally, see Richard Ketchum, "Plato on Real Being," *American Philosophical Quarterly* 17 (1980), pp. 213–20; Edward Lee, "Plato on Negation and Non-Being in the *Sophist*," *Philosophical Review* 81 (1972), pp. 267–304; and Paul Seligman, *Being and Not-Being: An Introduction to Plato's* Sophist (The Hague: Nijhoff, 1974).

2. A. E. Taylor, *Plato: The Man and His Work* (New York: Dial, 1936), pp. 384–85. Whitehead had a great deal of admiration for Taylor, however, especially regarding the *Timaeus*, as is evidenced in his references to Taylor in *Process and Reality* and *Adventures of Ideas*.

3. J. N. Findlay, *Plato: The Written and Unwritten Doctrines*, p. 263.

4. Cornford relies here on Joseph Souilhe, *Etude sur le terme "Dynamis" dans les dialogues de Platon* (Paris: Alcan, 1919). Souilhe is especially good on the technical

significance of *dynamis* in medicine, say in the Hippocratic tract *On Ancient Medicine*. Also see *Charmides* (156B) and the *Timaeus* (32C, 66A, 82E, 85D) regarding several medicinal *dynameis*. Finally, see Paul Pritchard, "The Meaning of *Dynamis* at *Timaeus* 31C," *Phronesis* 35 (1990), pp. 182–93.

5. Regarding passive *dynamis* in sensation, see *Republic* (507C, 509B), *Phaedrus* (270B), and *Theaetetus* (156A).

6. See F. M. Cornford, *Plato's Theory of Knowledge* (London: Kegan Paul, 1935), pp. 234–39.

7. Alfred North Whitehead, *Adventures of Ideas* (New York: Free Press, 1961), pp. 5–6, 25, 83, 118–22, 129, 166–69.

8. Alfred North Whitehead, *Modes of Thought* (New York: Macmillan, 1938), pp. 162–63.

9. Ibid., pp. 92, 112, 126, 132.

10. Alfred North Whitehead, *Adventures of Ideas*, pp. 83, 154, 158–59, 166, 275, 276.

11. See Alfred North Whitehead, *Science and the Modern World* (New York: Macmillan, 1957), pp. 234–35. Also see *Dialogues of Alfred North Whitehead* (Boston: Little, Brown 1954), p. 217.

12. Leonard Eslick, "The Platonic Dialectic of Non-Being," *New Scholasticism* 29 (1955), p. 45. Also see David Bostock, "Plato on Change and Time in the *Parmenides*," *Phronesis* 23 (1978), pp. 229–42; and Kenneth Sayre, "Plato's *Parmenides*: Why the Eight Hypotheses Are Not Contradictory," *Phronesis* 23 (1978), pp. 133–50.

13. See William Christian, *An Interpretation of Whitehead's Metaphysics* (New Haven: Yale University Press, 1959), pp. 246, 252, on the importance of the mingling of forms in Whitehead, even if the form when seen *in itself* does not mingle; but a form is not so much a one-in-itself as a one-as-being (as power). It should be noted that, on the evidence of the *Parmenides*, if the one is simply one and nothing can be predicated of it, then apophatic or negative theology would seem to be the only religious alternative open to us. See Sherwin Klein, "Plato's *Parmenides* and St. Thomas's Analysis of God as One and Trinity," *The Thomist* 55 (1991), pp. 229–44.

14. Leonard Eslick, "The Platonic Dialectic of Non-Being," p. 49; also see pp. 42–44, 46–48.

15. Leonard Eslick, "The Dyadic Character of Being in Plato," *Modern Schoolman* 31 (1953), p. 17.

16. See Victor Lowe, *Understanding Whitehead* (Baltimore: Johns Hopkins University Press, 1962), p. 27. Lowe is skeptical as to whether as many of Whitehead's ideas can be traced back to Plato as Whitehead thought could be; also

see pp. 253–54, 268. The present chapter is meant in part to defend Whitehead's intuitions regarding Plato. Finally, see pp. 45–46, 327, 339.

17.   Josiah Royce, *The Philosophy of Loyalty* (New York: Macmillan, 1908), p. 11.

18.   Robert Neville, *Recovery of the Measure* (Albany: State University of New York Press, 1989), pp. 217–18; also see p. 108. On the concept of 'function as power' and of 'self-structuring power' in Hegel, see Neville's *God the Creator* (Chicago: University of Chicago Press, 1968), pp. 22, 28–35, 78–79.

19.   Robert Neville, *A Theology Primer* (Albany: State University of New York Press, 1991), p. 79.

20.   Robert Neville, *Soldier, Sage, Saint* (New York: Fordham University Press, 1978), pp. 89–91.

21.   Lewis Hahn, ed., *The Philosophy of Charles Hartshorne* (LaSalle, IL: Open Court, 1991).

22.   Charles Hartshorne, *Man's Vision of God*, p. 89; also see pp. xvi, 14.

23.   Ibid., pp. 198–99.

24.   Ibid., p. 294; also see pp. 205, 232, 244. It should be noted that Hartshorne, a lifelong feminist, later showed regret for using the male pronoun in reference to God in his earlier writings.

25.   See my "Hartshorne and Plato" in Lewis Hahn, ed., *The Philosophy of Charles Hartshorne*, pp. 465–87, and Hartshorne's reply on pp. 703–04.

26.   See Charles Hartshorne, *Insights and Oversights of Great Thinkers*, p. 367. Also see Hartshorne's *Omnipotence and Other Theological Mistakes*.

27.   See, e.g., Alfred North Whitehead, *Adventures of Ideas*, p. 169. Also see Blair Campbell, "Deity and Human Agency in Plato's *Laws*," *History of Political Thought* 2 (1981), pp. 417–46, on human agency in politics that is at odds with theological determinism.

28.   Robert Neville, *God the Creator*, p. 196; also see pp. 114–15.

29.   Ibid., p. 291. Also see Neville, *Recovery of the Measure*, p. 114.

30.   See *Plato's Sophist*, tr. Seth Bernadete (Chicago: University of Chicago Press, 1986), commentary on 247E.

31.   See Paul Weiss, *Reality* (Princeton: Princeton University Press, 1938), pp. 211, 269; *The God We Seek* (Carbondale: Southern Illinois University Press, 1964), pp. 92–93, 96; *Modes of Being* (Carbondale: Southern Illinois University Press, 1958), pp. 115, 222–23, 325, 343–44, 489, 493.

32.   See my "Rorty on Plato as an Edifier," in Peter Hare, ed., *Doing Philosophy Historically* (Buffalo: Prometheus Books, 1988). Also see Gordon Neal, ed., *Plato's*

Sophist (Manchester: Manchester University Press, 1975); and William Bondeson, "Non-Being and the One," *Apeiron* 7 (1973), pp. 13–21.

33.   See David Ray Griffin, *Reenchantment without Supernaturalism: A Process Philosophy of Religion* (Ithaca: Cornell University Press, 2001), pp. 103, 167, 260; Jon Levenson, *Creation and the Persistence of Evil: The Jewish Drama of Divine Omnipotence* (San Francisco: Harper and Row, 1988); and Gerhard May, *Creatio ex Nihilo: The Doctrine of "Creation out of Nothing" in Early Christian Thought* (Edinburgh: Clark, 1994).

34.   See Charles Hartshorne, *The Zero Fallacy and Other Essays in Neoclassical Metaphysics*, p. 72. Also see William Christian, *An Interpretation of Whitehead's Metaphysics*, p. 390; Victor Lowe, *Understanding Whitehead*, p. 112; and Alfred North Whitehead, *Adventures of Ideas*, pp. 166–67. Finally, see my *Divine Beauty: The Aesthetics of Charles Hartshorne*.

35.   See Charles Hartshorne, *Insights and Oversights of Great Thinkers*, pp. 26–27. Also see Norman Geisler, *Philosophy of Religion* (Grand Rapids: Zondervan, 1974), p. 334. On Plato and Christianity see Adam Fox, *Plato and the Christians* (New York: Philosophical Library, 1957).

36.   See Charles Hartshorne, *Whitehead's View of Reality* (New York: Pilgrim, 1981), p. 23.

37.   See Charles Hartshorne, *The Divine Relativity* (New Haven: Yale University Press, 1948), pp. 139, 142. Also see Hartshorne, *Insights and Oversights of Great Thinkers*, p. 367.

38.   See Diane O'Leary-Hawthorne, "Not-Being and Linguistic Deception," *Apeiron* 29 (1996), pp. 165–98. Also see Alfred North Whitehead, *Adventures of Ideas*, pp. 222–23, 237; and *Modes of Thought*, p. 74. Finally, see two analytic studies in Gregory Vlastos, ed., *Plato*, vol. 1 (Garden City, NY: Anchor Books, 1970): G. E. L. Owen, "Plato on Not-Being," pp. 223–67; and David Wiggins, "Sentence Meaning, Negation, and Plato's Problem of Non-Being," pp. 268–303.

39.   See Martin Heidegger, *Plato's Sophist* (Bloomington: Indiana University Press, 1997), pp. 328–30. Also see Hermann Bonitz, *Platonische Studien* (Berlin: Vahlen, 1886), p. 203; and Walter Brogan, "Heidegger's Aristotelian Reading of Plato," *Research in Phenomenology* 25 (1995), pp. 274–82. Brogan understands Heidegger to be saying that the definition of being in the *Sophist* points toward Aristotle. Further, see John Ellis, "*Dynamis* and Being: Heidegger on Plato's *Sophist* 247d8–e4," *Epoche* 3 (1995), pp. 43–78, where the author holds that whereas Paul Natorp rejects the definition of being as Plato's own, Heidegger takes the definition to be Plato's, but Heidegger thinks that the definition is another instance of Plato's "remarkable unclarity." On Natorp see *Platos Ideenlehre* (Hamburg: Meiner, 1961). The definition of being as dynamic power is seen as a gratuitous preontology by John Berry, "A Deconstruction of Plato's 'Battle of Gods and Giants,'" *Southwest Philosophy Review* 3 (1986), pp. 28–39. Finally, see

Derek Simon, "The *Sophist*, 246A–259E: *Ousia* and *to On* in Plato's Ontologies," *De Philosophia* 12 (1995–1996), pp. 155–77.

40.   Cf. one odd passage in the *Laws* (780E) where the Athenian speaks of providential necessity (*ek theias tinos anangkes*).

Notes to Chapter Three

1.   Harry Wolfson, "Extradeical and Intradeical Interpretations of Platonic Ideas," in *Religious Philosophy* (Cambridge: Harvard University Press, 1961).

2.   See David Ray Griffin, "Hartshorne's Differences from Whitehead," in Lewis Ford, ed., *Two Process Philosophers: Hartshorne's Encounter with Whitehead* (Tallahassee: American Academy of Religion, 1973).

3.   See Charles Hartshorne, *Insights and Oversights of Great Thinkers*, pp. 23–24.

4.   Charles Hartshorne, *Creative Synthesis and Philosophic Method*, pp. 121–22.

5.   See Charles Hartshorne, *Whitehead's Philosophy*, p. 76.

6.   Charles Hartshorne, *Beyond Humanism* (Lincoln: University of Nebraska Press, 1968), p. 148; also *Insights and Oversights of Great Thinkers*, p. 230.

7.   See Charles Hartshorne, *Whitehead's Philosophy*, p. 97.

8.   Charles Hartshorne, *Man's Vision of God*, p. 324.

9.   See Charles Hartshorne, *The Divine Relativity*, p. 120.

10.   See Charles Hartshorne, *Man's Vision of God*, p. 28.

11.   See Charles Hartshorne, *Insights and Oversights of Great Thinkers*, p. 38. Also see Stephen Korner, *What Is Philosophy?* (London: Penguin, 1969), p. 255.

12.   Charles Hartshorne, *Philosophers Speak of God*, pp. 56–57.

13.   See Charles Hartshorne, *Creative Synthesis and Philosophic Method*, pp. 22, 100.

14.   Ibid., pp. 59, 64. Also see Hartshorne, *Creativity in American Philosophy*, p. 276.

15.   See my *Plato's Philosophy of History* (Washington, DC: University Press of America, 1981). The above quotation is from Charles Hartshorne's review of this book in *Process Studies* 12 (1982), pp. 201–02.

16.   See David Ray Griffin, "Hartshorne's Differences from Whitehead," pp. 39–40.

17.   See, e.g., Lewis Ford, "Whitehead's Differences from Hartshorne," in Lewis Ford, ed., *Two Process Philosophers*. Also see Ivor Leclerc, "Whitehead and

the Theory of Form," in William Reese, ed., *Process and Divinity: The Hartshorne Festschrift* (LaSalle, IL: Open Court, 1964). Finally, see A. W. Levi, "Bergson or Whitehead?" in William Reese, ed., *Process and Divinity: The Hartshorne Festschrift*.

18.   Charles Hartshorne, *Whitehead's Philosophy*, pp. 153, 186–87. Also see Leonidas Bargeliotes, "Whitehead's Double Debt to Plato," *Diotima* 12 (1984), pp. 33–40.

19.   Charles Hartshorne, *Whitehead's View of Reality* (New York: Pilgrim, 1981), p. 9.

20.   Charles Hartshorne, *Insights and Oversights of Great Thinkers*, p. 34. Also see Hartshorne, *Creative Synthesis and Philosophic Method*, p. 225.

21.   See David Ray Griffin, *Reenchantment without Supernaturalism: A Process Philosophy of Religion*, pp. 39–40, 159, 191–92. Also see Penelope Maddy, *Realism in Mathematics* (Oxford: Clarendon, 1990). Finally, see Reuben Hersh, *What Is Mathematics, Really?* (New York: Oxford University Press, 1997).

22.   David Ray Griffin, *Reenchantment without Supernaturalism: A Process Philosophy of Religion*, pp. 173, 210–11, 249, 266, 351. Also see James Feibleman, *Religious Platonism* (London: Allen and Unwin, 1959). Finally, see John Kenny, *Mystical Monotheism: A Study in Ancient Platonic Theology* (Hanover, NH: University Press of New England, 1991).

23.   See Charles Hartshorne, *The Zero Fallacy and Other Essays in Neoclassical Metaphysics*, p. 126. The insert is mine; I think it makes this quotation from Hartshorne consistent with what he says elsewhere.

24.   See Alfred North Whitehead, *Process and Reality*, pp. 43–44, 46; see the many references to "eternal objects" in the index. Also see William Christian, *An Interpretation of Whitehead's Metaphysics*, pp. 136, 194, 196–200, 208, 258. Finally, see the magisterial work by J. B. Skemp, *The Theory of Motion in Plato's Later Dialogues* (Amsterdam: Hakkert, 1967).

25.   See Victor Lowe, *Understanding Whitehead*, pp. 140, 143, 251, 327.

26.   See Alfred North Whitehead, *Science and the Modern World*, pp. 29–30. Also see Donald Sherburne, *A Key to Whitehead's Process and Reality* (New York: Macmillan, 1966), pp. 220–22. Finally, see Roy Wood Sellars, "Philosophy of Organism and Physical Realism," in P. A. Schilpp, ed., *The Philosophy of Alfred North Whitehead*, p. 411.

27.   See Charles Hartshorne, *The Divine Relativity*, p. 126. Also see Hartshorne, *Philosophers Speak of God*, pp. 22–24. Finally, see George Shields, ed., *Process and Analysis: Essays on Whitehead, Hartshorne, and the Analytic Tradition* (Albany: State University of New York Press, 2003).

28.   See Alfred North Whitehead, *Modes of Thought*, pp. 92–93, 126. Also see A. E. Taylor, "Whitehead's Philosophy of Religion," *The Dublin Review* 181

(July, 1927), p. 31; Eric Perl, "The Demiurge and the Forms: A Return to the Ancient Interpretation of Plato's Forms," *Ancient Philosophy* 18 (1998), pp. 81–92; and Eugenio Benitez, "The Good or the Demiurge," *Apeiron* 28 (1995), pp. 113–40. Finally, see Stephen Menn, "Aristotle and Plato on God as *Nous* and as the Good," *Review of Metaphysics* 45 (1992), pp. 543–73.

29. See Michael Morgan, *Platonic Piety* (New Haven: Yale University Press, 1990), who treats piety in Plato's early and middle dialogues; also see Morgan, "Plato and Greek Religion," in Richard Kraut, ed., *The Cambridge Companion to Plato.* Also see Dominic O'Meara, *Neoplatonism and Christian Thought* (Albany: State University of New York Press, 1982); Daniel Anderson and Joseph Brent, "The Questioning of the Existence of the Forms in Plato's *Timaeus,*" *Tulane Studies in Philosophy* 27 (1978), pp. 1–12; and Jon Mikalson, *Athenian Popular Religion* (Chapel Hill: University of North Carolina Press, 1983).

30. See Werner Jaeger, *The Theology of the Early Greek Philosophers* (Oxford: Oxford University Press, 1947). Also see Martin Nilsson, *A History of Greek Religion* (Oxford: Oxford University Press, 1952).

NOTES TO CHAPTER FOUR

1. Charles Hartshorne, *Philosophers Speak of God*, p. 4.

2. Ibid., p. 2.

3. Ibid., p. 15. Also see my *St. John of the Cross* (Albany: State University of New York Press, 1992).

4. Charles Hartshorne, *Philosophers Speak of God*, p. 3.

5. Ibid., p. 4. Also see Hartshorne, *Insights and Oversights of Great Thinkers*, p. 55.

6. See my "Was Plato a Vegetarian?" *Apeiron* 18 (1984), pp. 1–9; also see my *Philosophy of Vegetarianism* (Amherst: University of Massachusetts Press, 1984).

7. Charles Hartshorne, *Philosophers Speak of God*, pp. 14–15.

8. Ibid., p. 24. Also see Kevin Doherty, "The Demiurge and the Good in Plato," *New Scholasticism* 35 (1961), pp. 510–24; and David Keyt, "The Mad Craftsman of the Timaeus," *Philosophical Review* 80 (1971), pp. 230–35, who is instructive regarding Plato's theodicy.

9. See Charles Hartshorne, *Insights and Oversights of Great Thinkers*, p. 366.

10. Ibid., p. 54. Also see Robert Brumbaugh, *Unreality and Time* (Albany: State University of New York Press, 1984); W. C. Kneale, "Time and Eternity in Theology," *Proceedings of the Aristotelian Society* 61 (1961), pp. 87–108; and

Nathaniel Lawrence, "The Vision of Beauty and the Temporality of Deity in Whitehead's Philosophy," *Journal of Philosophy* 58 (1961), pp. 535–52.

11.   See Charles Hartshorne, "God and the Meaning of Life," in Leroy Rouner, ed., *On Nature* (Notre Dame: University of Notre Dame Press, 1984), pp. 154–68, especially p. 158. Also see Leonard Eslick, "The Dyadic Character of Being in Plato," pp. 11–18; and James Reagan, "Being and Nonbeing in Plato's *Sophist*," *Modern Schoolman* 42 (1965), pp. 305–14.

12.   Charles Hartshorne, *Creative Synthesis and Philosophic Method*, pp. 307–08. Also see Robert Brumbaugh, *The Role of Mathematics in Plato's Dialectic* (Chicago: University of Chicago Libraries, 1942).

13.   See Charles Hartshorne, *Philosophers Speak of God*, pp. 2, 5. Also see William Reese, "Dipolarity and Monopolarity in the Idea of God," *Dialogos* 18 (1983), pp. 51–58.

14.   See F. M. Cornford, *Plato's Cosmology* (London: Routledge and Kegan Paul, 1937), p. 39, who claims that in the divine soul of the universe is a divine reason, the latter symbolized by the Demiurge. Also see Charles Hartshorne, *Aquinas to Whitehead* (Milwaukee: Marquette University Press, 1976), pp. 4–5; and *Insights and Oversights of Great Thinkers*, pp. 70–71.

15.   See Charles Hartshorne, *Philosophers Speak of God*, pp. 39–40, 43.

16.   See P. E. More, *The Religion of Plato*, p. 120. Also see A. Boyce Gibson, "The Two Strands in Natural Theology," in William Reese, ed., *Process and Divinity: The Hartshorne Festschrift*, pp. 472, 475–76.

17.   See Charles Hartshorne, *Philosophers Speak of God*, p. 54. Also see Joseph Brennan, "Whitehead on Time and Endurance," *Southern Journal of Philosophy* 12 (1974), pp. 117–26; David Kolb, "Time and the Timeless in Greek Thought," *Philosophy East and West* 24 (1974), pp. 137–43; and Robert Bolton, "Plato's Distinction between Being and Becoming," *Review of Metaphysics* 29 (1975), pp. 66–95.

18.   See Charles Hartshorne, *Philosophers Speak of God*, p. 357.

19.   See Harry Wolfson, *The Philosophy of Spinoza* (Cambridge: Harvard University Press, 1934), 1, pp. 358–60.

20.   See Charles Hartshorne, *Philosophers Speak of God*, pp. 31, 56; also see Hartshorne, *Aquinas to Whitehead*, pp. 4–5, 30.

21.   See Charles Hartshorne, *Creative Synthesis and Philosophic Method*, pp. 69, 229.

22.   Charles Hartshorne, *Anselm's Discovery*, p. 232.

23.   Charles Hartshorne, *The Divine Relativity*, pp. 79–80.

24.   See Charles Hartshorne, *Beyond Humanism*, pp. 27–28, 63, 276.

25.   Charles Hartshorne, *Whitehead's Philosophy*, p. 167; also see Hartshorne, *Omnipotence and Other Theological Mistakes*, pp. 2–3.

26.   See Charles Hartshorne, *Insights and Oversights of Great Thinkers*, pp. 27–28; also see Hartshorne, *Creativity in American Philosophy*, pp. 208–09.

27.   See Charles Hartshorne, *Insights and Oversights of Great Thinkers*, pp. 32–33. Also see David Keyt, "Plato's Paradox That the Immutable Is Unknowable," *Philosophical Quarterly* 19 (1969), pp. 1–14.

28.   Charles Hartshorne, *Anselm's Discovery*, p. 289.

29.   See Charles Hartshorne, *Philosophers Speak of God*, pp. 58–59. In addition to the standard texts where Aristotle discusses the gods, consider *De anima* 406B, where he appears to criticize Plato's attempt in the *Timaeus* to think of the World Soul animating the spatial magnitude of the body of the world.

30.   Cf., Michel Despland, *The Education of Desire: Plato and the Philosophy of Religion* (Toronto: University of Toronto Press, 1985), where the author sees the shift from Platonic theism to Christianity as being primarily characterized by two different attitudes toward eros, with Plato facing its reality more forthrightly than Christianity. Also see Helmut Maassen, "Revelation, Myth, and Metaphysics: Three Traditional Concepts of God and Whitehead's Dipolar God," *Process Studies* 23 (1994), pp. 1–9.

31.   See William Christian, *An Interpretation of Whitehead's Metaphysics*, p. 387; Victor Lowe, *Understanding Whitehead*, pp. 47, 339; and Rem Edwards, "The Pagan Dogma of the Absolute Unchangeableness of God," *Religious Studies* 14 (1978), pp. 305–13, who argues that divine immutability was not a biblical doctrine, but came from Parmenides, Plato, and Aristotle. On the history of the identification of *ousia* and God, see George Stead, *Divine Substance* (Oxford: Clarendon, 1977). Finally, see Alfred North Whitehead, *Adventures of Ideas*, p. 275.

32.   See Charles Hartshorne, *Existence and Actuality* (Chicago: University of Chicago Press, 1984).

33.   See Steven Schoenly, "The Etymologies of the Names of the Gods: *Cratylus* 400D–404B," *Dialogue* 16 (1974), pp. 44–53.

34.   See Randall Auxier and Mark Davies, eds., *Hartshorne and Brightman on God, Process, and Persons: The Correspondence, 1922–1945*, pp. 87, 93–94, 113.

35.   See Ivor Leclerc, "The Metaphysics of the Good," *Review of Metaphysics* 35 (1981), pp. 11, 17, 20. Also see Julius Bixler, "Whitehead's Philosophy of Religion," in P. A. Schilpp, ed., *The Philosophy of Alfred North Whitehead*, pp. 489–511, especially pp. 491, 503.

36.   See Charles Hartshorne, *The Zero Fallacy and Other Essays in Neoclassical Metaphysics*, p. 164; also see pp. 62, 69, 87, 103, 165, 212. Finally, see Alfred North Whitehead, *Process and Reality*, pp. 94, 209, 346.

NOTES TO CHAPTER FIVE

1. Mattias Esser, *Der ontologische Gottesbeweis und seine Geschichte* (Bonn: Buchdruckerei von Seb. Foppen, 1905).

2. Leonard Eslick, "Plato's Dialectic of the Sun," in Linus Thro, ed., *History of Philosophy in the Making* (Washington, DC: University Press of America, 1982), p. 21.

3. Ibid., p. 23. The added comment in brackets better indicates Eslick's own view, I think.

4. Ibid., p. 27.

5. See J. Prescott Johnson, "The Ontological Argument in Plato," *The Personalist* 44 (1963), pp. 24–34.

6. See Charles Hartshorne, *Anselm's Discovery*, pp. 139–40, 149.

7. See J. Prescott Johnson, "The Ontological Argument in Plato," p. 29.

8. Ibid., p. 31.

9. On the global argument for the existence of God, see Charles Hartshorne, *Creative Synthesis and Philosophic Method*. A good secondary source is Donald Viney, *Charles Hartshorne and the Existence of God* (Albany: State University of New York Press, 1985). Also see Leonard Peikoff, "Platonism's Inference from Logic to God," *International Studies in Philosophy* 16 (1984), pp. 25–34, who argues that laws of logic, as in the law of noncontradiction that is true in any possible world, presuppose the existence of a divine mind. Finally, see two articles by Antonio Mesquita that deal with what amounts to an ontological argument in the *Phaedo* (102–07): "O Argumento Ontologico em Platao, I," *Philosophica* (1993), pp. 31–42; and "O Argumento Ontologico em Platao, II," *Philosophica* (1994), pp. 85–109.

10. See, e.g., John Baillie, *The Sense of the Presence of God* (New York: Scribner's, 1962), p. 122. The label *natural theology*, however, was invented by Cicero's contemporary Marcus Terentius Varro. See A. E. Taylor, *Platonism and Its Influence* (New York: Longmans, Green, 1932), p. 99.

11. See, e.g., A. H. Armstrong and R. A. Markus, *Christian Faith and Greek Philosophy* (New York: Sheed and Ward, 1960).

12. See Chung-Hwan Chen, "Plato's Theistic Teleology," *Anglican Theological Review* 43 (1961), pp. 71–87. John Wild points out that this teleological argument is found in a weak way in several dialogues, including the *Timaeus* (29, 47) and the *Philebus* (28). See Wild's "Plato and Christianity," *The Journal of Bible and Religion* 17 (1949), especially p. 9. Also see Gerard Watson, "The Theology of Plato and Aristotle," *Irish Theological Quarterly* 37 (1970), p. 60.

13. For outlines of this version of the cosmological argument in Plato, see William Lane Craig, *The Cosmological Argument from Plato to Leibniz*, p. 4; and Norman Geisler, *Philosophy of Religion*, pp. 163–64.

14. See Plato, *Laws*, tr. A. E. Taylor (London: Dent, 1934).

15. William Lane Craig, *The Cosmological Argument from Plato to Leibniz*, p. 7. Cf. W. F. R. Hardie, *A Study in Plato* (Oxford: Clarendon, 1936), pp. 107–08, who interprets Plato's argument in terms of temporal priority.

16. William Lane Craig, *The Cosmological Argument from Plato to Leibniz*, p. 8. Also see Friedrich Solmsen, *Plato's Theology*, pp. 89, 92; and G. M. A. Grube, *Plato's Thought*, p. 122.

17. J. B. Skemp, *The Theory of Motion in Plato's Later Dialogues*, p. 68.

18. See my "On Taking Polytheism Seriously," *Buddhist-Christian Studies* 14 (1994), pp. 127–35.

19. G. M. A. Grube, *Plato's Thought*, pp. 150–51. Also see A. E. Taylor, *Platonism and Its Influence*, p. 103.

20. William Lane Craig, *The Cosmological Argument from Plato to Leibniz*, p. 11. Once again, P. E. More is not helpful in his suggestion that if the World Soul were God, pantheism would result. Pan*en*theism is an option he does not consider. See P. E. More, *The Religion of Plato*, pp. 222–23. Also see F. M. Cornford, *The "Polytheism" of Plato* (Oxford: Blackwell, 1938) and subsequent responses in A. E. Taylor, "The 'Polytheism' of Plato: An Apologia," *Mind* 47 (1938), pp. 183–84; and F. M. Cornford, "The 'Polytheism' of Plato: An Apology," *Mind* 47 (1938), p. 324. Finally, see Gustav Mueller, "Plato and the Gods," *Philosophical Review* 45 (1936), pp. 462–69.

21. Norman Geisler, *Philosophy of Religion*, pp. 164–65.

22. See, e.g., William Lane Craig, *The Cosmological Argument from Plato to Leibniz*, pp. 14–15. Also see Kevin Doherty, "The Location of the Platonic Ideas," *Review of Metaphysics* 14 (1960), pp. 57–72. Cf. Reginald Hackforth, "Plato's Theism," in R. E. Allen, ed., *Studies in Plato's Metaphysics* (London: Routledge and Kegan Paul, 1965), pp. 439–47. Finally, see Charles Bigger, "On the World Soul in Plato's *Timaeus*," *Southern Journal of Philosophy* 5 (1967), pp. 1–8.

23. Leonard Eslick, "From the World to God: The Cosmological Argument," *Modern Schoolman* 60 (1983), p. 165.

24. Leonard Eslick, "Plato's Dialectic of the Sun," p. 30; also see p. 32.

25. See James Feibleman, *Religious Platonism*; and John Rexine, *Religion in Plato and Cicero* (New York: Philosophical Library, 1959).

26. See Charles Hartshorne, *Anselm's Discovery*, pp. 57–59. Also see A. Boyce Gibson, "Change and Continuity in Plato's Thought," *Review of Metaphysics*

11 (1957), pp. 237–55. Hartshorne also relies on Julius Stenzel, *Plato's Method of Dialectic*.

27.   Charles Hartshorne, *A Natural Theology for Our Time*, p. 125. Also see Hartshorne's *Philosophers Speak of God*, p. 25.

28.   See my *Divine Beauty: The Aesthetics of Charles Hartshorne*.

29.   See Charles Hartshorne, *Insights and Oversights of Great Thinkers*, pp. 36–38. Also see John Burnet, *Early Greek Philosophy*.

30.   See Charles Hartshorne, *Omnipotence and Other Theological Mistakes*, p. 53. Also see Raphael Demos, *The Philosophy of Plato*, especially pp. 120–25, who influenced Hartshorne's interpretation of Plato a great deal.

31.   See Charles Hartshorne, *Insights and Oversights of Great Thinkers*, pp. x–xi.

32.   See Charles Hartshorne, *Creative Synthesis and Philosophic Method*, pp. 22, 159.

33.   Charles Hartshorne, *Anselm's Discovery*, pp. 139–41.

34.   Ibid., pp. 148–49, 307.

35.   Ibid., pp. 27–31.

36.   Ibid., pp. 50–59. Also see George Claghorn, *Aristotle's Criticism of Plato's "Timaeus"* (The Hague: Nijhoff, 1954).

37.   Charles Hartshorne, *Anselm's Discovery*, pp. 50–59.

38.   Ibid.

Notes to Chapter Six

1.   Throughout this section of the chapter I rely on Robert Carter, "Plato and Mysticism," *Idealistic Studies* 5 (1975), pp. 255–68.

2.   William James, *The Varieties of Religious Experience* (Cambridge: Harvard University Press, 1985).

3.   Walter Kauffman, *Critique of Religion and Philosophy* (Garden City, NY: Doubleday, 1961), p. 316.

4.   Henri Bergson, *The Two Sources of Morality and Religion* (Garden City, NY: Doubleday, 1935), p. 232.

5.   W. T. Stace, *Mysticism and Philosophy* (London: Macmillan, 1960), pp. 131–32.

6.   Paul Friedlander, *Plato*, pp. 71ff. Also see Glenn Morrow, "Necessity and Persuasion in Plato's *Timaeus*," *Philosophical Review* 59 (1950), pp. 147–63.

7. Bertrand Russell, "Knowledge by Acquaintance and Knowledge by Description," in *The Basic Writings of Bertrand Russell* (New York: Simon and Schuster, 1961), pp. 217–24.

8. Alfred North Whitehead, *The Function of Reason*, p. 11; also see pp. 10, 12, 37–38, 83–84.

9. Alfred North Whitehead, *Adventures of Ideas*, pp. 45–59. Also see Whitehead's "Mathematics and the Good," in P. A. Schilpp, ed., *The Philosophy of Alfred North Whitehead*, pp. 666–81.

10. Aldous Huxley, *Time Must Have a Stop* (New York: Harper and Row, 1965), p. 225. Also see W. K. C. Guthrie, *The Greeks and Their Gods* (London: Methuen, 1950).

11. Hazel Barnes, "Apotheosis and Deification in Plato, Nietzsche, and Huxley," *Philosophy and Literature* 1 (1976), pp. 3–24.

12. See my "Asceticism and Athletic Training in Plotinus," *Aufstieg und Niedergang der Romischen Welt* 36 (1987), pp. 701–12. Also see Kevin Doherty, "God and the Good in Plato," *New Scholasticism* 30 (1956), pp. 441–60, who is very good on the debate regarding whether the form of the good is God: both sides are partially correct in this debate if the form of the good is in the divine mind as the most exalted intellectual content, but it is not to be literally identified with God. Finally, see Alfred North Whitehead, *Modes of Thought*, pp. 171, 174.

13. David Sedley, "'Becoming like God' in the *Timaeus* and Aristotle," in Tomas Calvo and Luc Brisson, eds., *Interpreting the "Timaeus"—"Critias,"* pp. 327–39. Also see Sedley, "The Ideal of Godlikeness," in Gail Fine, ed., *Plato*, vol. 2 (Oxford: Oxford University Press, 1999). Also see Hubert Merki, *Homoiosis Theoi* (Freiburg: Paulusverlag, 1952); John Passmore, *The Perfectibility of Man* (London: Duckworth, 1970); and Julia Annas, *Platonic Ethics, Old and New* (Ithaca: Cornell University Press, 1999), ch. 3. Finally, Timothy Mahoney, in "Becoming like God in the *Timaeus*: A Critique of David Sedley's Interpretation," paper delivered at the APA convention, Washington, DC, December 29, 2003, argues that Plato's *homoiosis theoi* involves not only intellectual development but development of moral virtue as well.

14. John Armstrong, "Plato on Becoming like God: Flight or Fight?" paper delivered at the APA Convention, Chicago; April 26, 2002. In addition, see Friedrich Solmsen's *Plato's Theology*; and Kathleen Freeman, *God, Man, and State* (Boston: Beacon, 1952). Finally, see W. F. R. Hardie, *Aristotle's Ethical Theory* (Oxford: Clarendon, 1980); and John Herman Randall, *Aristotle* (New York: Columbia University Press, 1960), pp. 143–44. Randall is helpful regarding what Aristotle *should have said* regarding God in order to be consistent with his hylomorphism: God is the form of the world's matter and God is the *energeia* and *entelecheia* of its *dynameis*.

15.   See Martha Nussbaum, *The Fragility of Goodness* (Cambridge: Cambridge University Press, 1986), pp. 373–77. Also see Ronald Epp, "*Katharsis* and the Platonic Reconstruction of Mystical Terminology," *Philosophia* 4 (1974), pp. 168–79.

16.   See James Duerlinger, "Ethics and the Divine Life in Plato's Philosophy," *Journal of Religious Ethics* 13 (1985), pp. 312–31.

17.   See J. V. Luce, "Plato's Religious Experience," *Hermathena* 96 (1962), pp. 73–91. Also see Culbert Rutenber, *The Doctrine of the Imitation of God in Plato* (New York: King's Crown, 1946); and John Wild, "Review of *The Doctrine of the Imitation of God in Plato*," *Journal of Religion* 29 (1949), p. 75.

18.   See Kenneth Seeskin, "Platonism, Mysticism, and Madness," *Monist* 59 (1976), pp. 574–86; Erik Ostenfeld, "Self-Motion, Tripartition, and Embodiment," in Livio Rossetti, ed., *Understanding the "Phaedrus,"* pp. 324–28; David Johnson, "God as the True Self," *Ancient Philosophy* 19 (1999), pp. 1–19; Andre Festugiere, *Personal Religion among the Greeks* (Berkeley: University of California Press, 1954); and Conrado Eggers Lan, "Zeus e Anima del Mondo nel *Fedro* (246E–253C)," in Livio Rossetti, ed., *Understanding the "Phaedrus,"* pp. 40–46.

19.   See John Carmody, "Plato's Religious Horizon," *Philosophy Today* 15 (1971), pp. 52–68. Carmody does not see Plato's God as personal; CF. A. E. Taylor, *Plato: The Man and His Work*, pp. 441–42, 489–94. Carmody relies a great deal on Eric Voegelin, *Order and History*, vol. 3 (Baton Rouge: Louisiana State University Press, 1957), pp. 3–268.

20.   See Ulrich von Wilamowitz-Moellendorff, *Platon*, vol. 1 (Berlin: Weidmann, 1920), p. 348.

21.   See Norman Pittinger, *Catholic Faith in a Process Perspective* (Maryknoll, NY: Orbis Books, 1981), p. 27.

22.   See David Sedley, "The Ideal of Godlikeness," in Gail Fine, ed., *Plato*, vol. 2, pp. 309–28.

23.   Ibid., p. 314.

24.   Ibid., p. 316.

25.   Ibid., p. 323; also see pp. 320, 322, 324–25.

26.   Julia Annas, *Platonic Ethics, Old and New*, ch. 3.

27.   Annas relies on Rachel Rue, "The Philosopher in Flight: The Digression (172C–177C) in the *Theaetetus*," *Oxford Studies in Ancient Philosophy* 10 (1993), pp. 71–100.

28.   See Julia Annas, *Platonic Ethics, Old and New*, especially pp. 53, 64.

29.   See Eric Havelock, *Preface to Plato* (Cambridge: Harvard University Press, 1963).

30. See Charles Hartshorne, "Mysticism and Rationalistic Metaphysics," *Monist* 59 (1976), pp. 463–69.

31. Ibid., p. 463.

32. Ibid., p. 467. Also see George Santayana, *Platonism and the Spiritual Life* (New York: Scribner's, 1927). It should be noted that in Hartshorne's private library can be found a marked copy of Sain Jean de la Croix, *La Montee du Carmel* (Paris: De Brouwer, 1922), indicating Hartshorne's familiarity with the Catholic mystical tradition.

33. See Burton Cooper, *The Idea of God* (The Hague: Nijhoff, 1974), pp. 95–118, although it should be noted that Cooper, despite the fact that he is a process theist, interprets Plato as a precursor to classical theism.

34. See William Wordsworth, "The Tables Turned" and "Sonnet XXXIII," in *Poetical Works* (Oxford: Oxford University Press, 1981).

35. Ibid., "Intimations of Immortality from Recollections of Early Childhood."

36. In this paragraph I have relied again on Burton Cooper, *The Idea of God*, pp. 102–10.

37. Culbert Rutenber, *The Doctrine of the Imitation of God in Plato*, p. 42. This work was Rutenber's doctoral dissertation at the University of Pennsylvania.

38. Ibid., p. 8, for a list of such scholars.

39. Ibid., p. 13. Also see Ulrich von Wilamowitz-Moellendorff, *Platon*, vol. 1, pp. 589ff.

40. See Culbert Rutenber, *The Doctrine of the Imitation of God in Plato*, pp. 10, 32, for a list of famous scholars who concur with this judgment.

41. Ibid., p. 16.

42. Ibid., p. 37.

43. Ibid., pp. 52–53.

44. Ibid., pp. 56, 59, 68–69, 74, 93, 101. Also see Ernest Barker, *Greek Political Theory* (New York: Barnes and Noble, 1960), p. 204.

Bibliography

Anderson, Daniel, and Joseph Brent. "The Questioning of the Existence of the Forms in Plato's *Timaeus.*" *Tulane Studies in Philosophy* 27 (1978): 1–12.

Annas, Julia. *Platonic Ethics, Old and New.* Ithaca: Cornell University Press, 1999.

Armstrong, A. H., and R. A. Markus. *Christian Faith and Greek Philosophy.* New York: Sheed and Ward, 1960.

Armstrong, John. "Plato on Becoming like God: Flight or Fight?" Paper delivered to the APA Convention, Chicago; April 26, 2002.

Ashbaugh, Anne. *Plato's Theory of Explanation: A Study of the Cosmological Account in the "Timaeus."* Albany: State University of New York Press, 1988.

Baillie, John. *The Sense of the Presence of God.* New York: Scribner's, 1962.

Bargeliotes, Leonidas. "Whitehead's Double Debt to Plato." *Diotima* 12 (1984): 33–40.

———. "Divinized and De-divinized Conceptions of the World and of Cosmos." In Aphrodite Alexandrakis, ed., *Neoplatonism and Western Aesthetics.* Albany: State University of New York Press, 2002. Pp. 229–46.

Barker, Ernest. *Greek Political Theory.* New York: Barnes and Noble, 1960.

Barnes, Hazel. "Apotheosis and Deification in Plato, Nietzsche, and Huxley." *Philosophy and Literature* 1 (1976): 3–24.

Barnes, Jonathan. *The Presocratic Philosophers.* London: Routledge and Kegan Paul, 1979.

Beckman, James. *The Religious Dimension of Socrates' Thought.* Waterloo, Canada: Wildred Laurier University Press, 1979.

Benitez, Eugenio. "The Good or the Demiurge." *Apeiron* 28 (1995): 113–40.

Bergson, Henri. *The Two Sources of Morality and Religion.* Garden City, NY: Doubleday, 1935.

Berry, John. "A Deconstruction of Plato's 'Battle of Gods and Giants.'" *Southwest Philosophy Review* 3 (1986): 28–39.

Bigger, Charles. "On the World Soul in Plato's *Timaeus.*" *Southern Journal of Philosophy* 5 (1967): 1–8.

Bixler, Julius. "Whitehead's Philosophy of Religion." In P. A. Schilpp, ed., *The Philosophy of Alfred North Whitehead*. LaSalle, IL: Open Court, 1951. Pp. 489–511.

Bolton, Robert. "Plato's Distinction between Being and Becoming." *Review of Metaphysics* 29 (1975): 66–95.

Bondeson, William. "Non-Being and the One." *Apeiron* 7 (1973): 13–21.

Bonifazi, Conrad. *The Soul of the World: An Account of the Inwardness of Things*. Washington, DC: University Press of America, 1978.

Bonitz, Hermann. *Platonische Studien*. Berlin: Vahlen, 1886.

Bostock, David. "Plato on Change and Time in the *Parmenides*." *Phronesis* 23 (1978): 229–42.

Bovet, Pierre. *Le Dieu de Platon d'apres l'ordre chronologique des dialogues*. Geneve: Kundig, 1902.

Brandwood, Leonard. *The Chronology of Plato's Dialogues*. Cambridge: Cambridge University Press, 1990.

Brennan, Joseph. "Whitehead on Plato's Cosmology." *Journal of the History of Philosophy* 9 (1971): 67–78.

———. "Whitehead on Time and Endurance." *Southern Journal of Philosophy* 12 (1974): 117–26.

Brightman, Edgar. "Platonism." In Vergilius Ferm, ed., *An Encyclopedia of Religion*. New York: Philosophical Library, 1945.

Brogan, Walter. "Heidegger's Aristotelian Reading of Plato." *Research in Phenomenology* 25 (1995): 274–82.

Brumbaugh, Robert. *The Role of Mathematics in Plato's Dialectic*. Chicago: University of Chicago Libraries, 1942.

Burkert, Walter. *Greek Religion*. Cambridge: Harvard University Press, 1985.

Burnet, John. *Early Greek Philosophy*. London: Black, 1930.

Campbell, Blair. "Deity and Human Agency in Plato's *Laws*." *History of Political Thought* 2 (1981): 417–46.

Carmody, John. "Plato's Religious Horizon." *Philosophy Today* 15 (1971): 52–68.

Carter, Robert. "Plato and Mysticism." *Idealistic Studies* 5 (1975): 255–68.

Chen, Chung-Hwan. "Plato's Theistic Teleology." *Anglican Theological Review* 43 (1961): 71–87.

Christian, William. *An Interpretation of Whitehead's Metaphysics*. New Haven: Yale University Press, 1959.

Claghorn, George. *Aristotle's Criticism of Plato's "Timaeus."* The Hague: Nijhoff, 1954.

Cobb, John. *Transforming Christianity and the World*. Maryknoll, NY: Orbis, 1999.

Collins, James. *The Emergence of Philosophy of Religion*. New Haven: Yale University Press, 1967.

Cook, Patricia. "Neville's Use of Plato." In J. H. Chapman, ed., *Interpreting Neville*. Albany: State University of New York Press, 1999. Pp. 45–57.

Cooper, Burton. *The Idea of God*. The Hague: Nijhoff, 1974.

Cornford, F. M. *Greek Religious Thought*. London: Dent, 1923.

———. *Plato's Theory of Knowledge*. London: Kegan Paul, 1935.

———. *Plato's Cosmology*. London: Routledge and Kegan Paul, 1937.

———. *The "Polytheism" of Plato*. Oxford: Blackwell, 1938.

———. "The 'Polytheism' of Plato: An Apology." *Mind* 47 (1938): 324.

———. *Plato's "Timaeus."* Indianapolis: Bobbs-Merrill, 1959.

Craig, William Lane. *The Cosmological Argument from Plato to Leibniz*. New York: Barnes and Noble, 1980.

Demos, Raphael. *The Philosophy of Plato*. New York: Scribner's, 1939.

Despland, Michael. *The Education of Desire: Plato and the Philosophy of Religion*. Toronto: University of Toronto Press, 1985.

De Vries, Willem. "On *Sophist* 255B–E." *History of Philosophy Quarterly* 5 (1988): 385–94.

Doherty, Kevin. "God and the Good in Plato." *New Scholasticism* 30 (1956): 441–60.

———. "The Location of the Platonic Ideas." *Review of Metaphysics* 14 (1960): 57–72.

Dombrowski, Daniel. *Plato's Philosophy of History*. Washington, DC: University Press of America, 1981.

———. *The Philosophy of Vegetariansism*. Amherst: University of Massachusetts Press, 1984.

———. "Was Plato a Vegetarian?" *Apeiron* 18 (1984): 1–9.

———. "Asceticism as Athletic Training in Plotinus." *Aufstieg und Niedergang der Romischen Welt* 36 (1987): 701–12.

———. "An Anticipation of Hartshorne: Plotinus on *Daktylos* and the World Soul." *The Heythrop Journal* 29 (1988): 462–67.

———. "Does God Have a Body?" *The Journal of Speculative Philosophy* 2 (1988): 225–32.

———. "Rorty on Plato as an Edifier." In Peter Hare, ed., *Doing Philosophy Historically*. Buffalo: Prometheus Books, 1988. Pp. 73–84.

———. "Nature as Personal." *Philosophy and Theology* 5 (1990): 81–96.

———. "Hartshorne and Plato." In Lewis Hahn, ed., *The Philosophy of Charles Hartshorne*. LaSalle, IL: Open Court, 1991. Pp. 465–487, 703–04.

———. *St. John of the Cross*. Albany: State University of New York Press, 1992.

———. "On Taking Polytheism Seriously." *Buddhist-Christian Studies* 14 (1994): 127–35.

———. *Analytic Theism, Hartshorne, and the Concept of God*. Albany: State University of New York Press, 1996.

———. *Divine Beauty: The Aesthetics of Charles Hartshorne*. Nashville: Vanderbilt University Press, 2004.

Duerlinger, James. "Ethics and the Divine Life in Plato's Philosophy." *Journal of Religious Ethics* 13 (1985): 312–31.

———. "The Ontology of Plato's *Sophist*." *Modern Schoolman* 65 (1988): 151–84.

Edwards, Rem. "The Pagan Dogma of the Absolute Unchangeableness of God." *Religious Studies* 14 (1978): 305–13.

Ellis, John. "*Dynamis* and Being: Heidegger on Plato's *Sophist* 247d8–e4." *Epoche* 3 (1995): 43–78.

Enders, Markus. "Platons 'Theologie': Der Gott, die Gotter und das Gute." *Perspektiven-der-Philosophie* 25 (1999): 131–85.

Epp, Ronald. "*Katharsis* and the Platonic Reconstruction of Mystical Terminology." *Philosophia* 4 (1974): 168–79.

Eslick, Leonard. "The Dyadic Character of Being in Plato." *Modern Schoolman* 31 (1953): 11–18.

———. "The Platonic Dialectic of Non-Being." *New Scholasticism* 29 (1955): 33–49.

———. "Plato's Dialectic of the Sun." In Linus Thro, ed., *History of Philosophy in the Making*. Washington, DC: University Press of America, 1982. Pp. 19–34.

———. "From the World to God: The Cosmological Argument." *Modern Schoolman* 60 (1983): 145–69.

Esser, Mattias. *Der ontologische Gottesbeweis und seine Geschichte*. Bonn: Buchdruckerei von Seb. Foppen, 1905.

Eucalano, Brian. "The Universal Soul." *Dialogue* 21 (1978): 25–30.

Feibleman, James. *Religious Platonism*. London: Allen and Unwin, 1959.

Festugiere, Andre. *Personal Religion among the Greeks*. Berkeley: University of California Press, 1954.

Findlay, J. N. *Plato: The Written and Unwritten Doctrines*. New York: Humanities, 1974.

———. "The Three Hypostases of Platonism." *Review of Metaphysics* 28 (1975): 660–80.

Ford, Lewis. "Whitehead's Differences from Hartshorne." In Lewis Ford, ed. *Two Process Philosophers: Hartshorne's Encounter with Whitehead*. Tallahassee: American Academy of Religion, 1973. Pp. 58–83.

Fox, Adam. *Plato and the Christians*. New York: Philosophical Library, 1957.

Freeman, Kathleen. *God, Man, and State*. Boston: Beacon, 1952.

Friedlander, Paul. *Plato*. New York: Pantheon, 1958.

Gadamer, Hans-Georg. *Dialogue and Dialectic*. New Haven: Yale University Press, 1980.

———. "Religion and Religiosity in Socrates." *Proceedings of the Boston Area Colloquium in Ancient Philosophy* 1 (1985): 53–76.

Geisler, Norman. *Philosophy of Religion*. Grand Rapids: Zondervan, 1974.

Gibson, A. Boyce. "Change and Continuity in Plato's Thought." *Review of Metaphysics* 11 (1957): 237–55.

———. "The Two Strands in Natural Theology." In William Reese, ed., *Process and Divinity: The Hartshorne Festschrift*. LaSalle, IL: Open Court, 1964. Pp. 471–92.

Gill, Mary. "Matter and Flux in Plato's *Timaeus*." *Phronesis* 32 (1987): 34–53.

Griffin, David Ray. "Hartshorne's Differences from Whitehead." In Lewis Ford, ed. *Two Process Philosophers: Hartshorne's Encounter with Whitehead*. Tallahassee: American Academy of Religion, 1973. Pp. 35–57.

———. *Reenchantment without Supernaturalism: A Process Philosophy of Religion*. Ithaca: Cornell University Press, 2001.

Griswold, Charles, ed. *Platonic Writings, Platonic Readings*. New York: Routledge, 1988.

———. "Commentary on Sayre's 'Why Plato Never Had a Theory of Forms.'" *Proceedings of the Boston Area Colloquium in Ancient Philosophy* 9 (1993): 200–12.

———. "*E Pluribus Unum?* On the Platonic 'Corpus.'" *Ancient Philosophy* 19 (1999): 361–97.

Grube, G. M. A. *Plato's Thought*. London: Methuen, 1935.

Guthrie, W. K. C. *The Greeks and Their Gods*. London: Methuen, 1950.

————. *A History of Greek Philosophy*. 6 vols. Cambridge: Cambridge University Press, 1978.

Hack, R. K. *God in Greek Philosophy to the Time of Socrates*. Princeton: Princeton University Press, 1931.

Hackforth, Reginald. "Plato's Theism." In R. E. Allen, ed., *Studies in Plato's Metaphysics*. London: Routledge and Kegan Paul, 1965. Pp. 439–47.

Hadot, Pierre. *What Is Ancient Philosophy?* Cambridge: Harvard University Press, 2002.

Hahn, Lewis, ed. *The Philosophy of Charles Hartshorne*. LaSalle, IL: Open Court, 1991.

Hardie, W. F. R. *A Study in Plato*. Oxford: Clarendon, 1936.

————. *Aristotle's Ethical Theory*. Oxford: Clarendon, 1980.

Hartshorne, Charles. *Man's Vision of God*. New York: Harper's, 1941.

————. *The Divine Relativity*. New Haven: Yale University Press, 1948.

————. *Philosophers Speak of God*. Chicago: University of Chicago Press, 1953.

————. *Reality as Social Process*. Boston: Beacon, 1953.

————. *Anselm's Discovery*. LaSalle, IL: Open Court, 1965.

————. *A Natural Theology for Our Time*. LaSalle, IL: Open Court, 1967.

————. *Beyond Humanism*. Lincoln: University of Nebraska Press, 1968.

————. *Creative Synthesis and Philosophic Method*. LaSalle, IL: Open Court, 1970.

————. *Whitehead's Philosophy*. Lincoln: University of Nebraska Press, 1972.

————. *Aquinas to Whitehead*. Milwaukee: Marquette University Press, 1976.

————. "Mysticism and Rationalistic Metaphysics." *Monist* 59 (1976): 463–69.

————. *Whitehead's View of Reality*. New York: Pilgrim, 1981.

————. "Review of Daniel A. Dombrowski, *Plato's Philosophy of History*." *Process Studies* 12 (1982): 201–02.

————. *Insights and Oversights of Great Thinkers*. Albany: State University of New York Press, 1983.

————. *Creativity in American Philosophy*. Albany: State University of New York Press, 1984.

————. *Existence and Actuality*. Chicago: University of Chicago Press, 1984.

————. "God and the Meaning of Life." In Leroy Rouner, ed., *On Nature*. Notre Dame: University of Notre Dame Press, 1984. Pp. 154–68.

————. *Omnipotence and Other Theological Mistakes*. Albany: State University of New York Press, 1984.

———. *The Zero Fallacy and Other Essays in Neoclassical Metaphysics.* LaSalle, IL: Open Court, 1997.

———. *Hartshorne and Brightman on God, Process, and Persons: The Correspondence, 1922–1945.* Ed. Randall Auxier and Mark Davies. Nashville: Vanderbilt University Press, 2001.

Havelock, Eric. *Preface to Plato.* Cambridge: Harvard University Press, 1963.

Heidegger, Martin. *Plato's "Sophist."* Bloomington: Indiana University Press, 1997.

Henning, Brian. "A Genuine Ethical Universe: Beauty, Morality, and Nature in a Processive Cosmos." Ph.D. dissertation. Fordham University, 2002.

Hersh, Reuben. *What Is Mathematics, Really?* New York: Oxford University Press, 1997.

Howland, Jacob. "Re-Reading Plato: The Problem of Platonic Chronology." *Phoenix* 45 (1991): 189–214.

Huxley, Aldous. *Time Must Have a Stop.* New York: Harper and Row, 1965.

Jackson, Darrell. "The Prayers of Socrates." *Phronesis* 16 (1971): 14–37.

Jaeger, Werner. *The Theology of the Early Greek Philosophers.* Oxford: Oxford University Press, 1947.

James, William. *The Varieties of Religious Experience.* Cambridge: Harvard University Press, 1985.

Jean de la Croix, Sain. *La Montee du Carmel.* Paris: De Brouwer, 1922.

Johnson, David. "God as the True Self." *Ancient Philosophy* 19 (1999): 1–19.

Johnson, J. Prescott. "The Ontological Argument in Plato." *The Personalist* 44 (1963): 24–34.

Kahn, Charles. *The Art and Thought of Heraclitus.* Cambridge: Cambridge University Press, 1981.

———. *Plato and the Socratic Dialogue.* Cambridge: Cambridge University Press, 1996.

———. "Response to Griswold." *Ancient Philosophy* 20 (2000): 189–93.

Kauffman, Walter. *Critique of Religion and Philosophy.* Garden City, NY: Doubleday, 1961.

Kenny, John. *Mystical Monotheism: A Study in Ancient Platonic Theology.* Hanover, NH: University Press of New England, 1991.

Keyt, David. "Plato's Paradox That the Immutable Is Unknowable." *Philosophical Quarterly* 19 (1969): 1–14.

Klein, Sherwin. "Plato's *Parmenides* and St. Thomas's Analysis of God as One and Trinity." *The Thomist* 55 (1991): 229–44.

Kohak, Erazim. *The Embers and the Stars*. Chicago: University of Chicago Press, 1984.

Kolb, David. "Time and the Timeless in Greek Thought." *Philosophy East and West* 24 (1974): 137–43.

Korner, Stephen. *What Is Philosophy?* London: Penguin, 1969.

Kraut, Richard. "Introduction to the Study of Plato." In Richard Kraut, ed., *The Cambridge Companion to Plato*. Cambridge: Cambridge University Press, 1992. Pp. 1–50.

Lan, Conrado Eggers. "Zeus e Anima del Mondo nel *Fedro* (246E–253C)." In Livio Rossetti, ed., *Understanding the "Phaedrus."* Sankt Augustin, Germany: Academia Verlag, 1992. Pp. 40–46.

Leclerc, Ivor. "Whitehead and the Theory of Form." In William Reese, ed., *Process and Divinity: The Hartshorne Festschrift*. LaSalle, IL: Open Court, 1964. Pp. 127–37.

———. "The Metaphysics of the Good." *Review of Metaphysics* 35 (1981): 3–26.

Levenson, Jon. *Creation and the Persistence of Evil: The Jewish Drama of Divine Omnipotence*. San Francisco: Harper and Row, 1988.

Levi, A. W. "Bergson or Whitehead?" In William Reese, ed., *Process and Divinity: The Hartshorne Festschrift*. LaSalle, IL: Open Court, 1964. Pp. 139–59.

Levinson, Ronald. *In Defense of Plato*. Cambridge: Harvard University Press, 1953.

Lowe, Victor. *Understanding Whitehead*. Baltimore: Johns Hopkins University Press, 1962.

Luce, J. V. "Plato's Religious Experience." *Hermathena* 96 (1962): 73–91.

Maassen, Helmut. "Revelation, Myth, and Metaphysics: Three Traditional Concepts of God and Whitehead's Dipolar God." *Process Studies* 23 (1994): 1–9.

Maddy, Penelope. *Realism in Mathematics*. Oxford: Clarendon, 1990.

Mahoney, Timothy. "Becoming like God in the *Timaeus*: A Critique of David Sedley's Interpretation." Paper presented at the American Philosophical Association convention; Washington, DC; December 29, 2003.

May, Gerhard. *Creatio ex Nihilo: The Doctrine of "Creation out of Nothing" in Early Christian Thought*. Edinburgh: Clark, 1994.

Mayr, Ernst. "A Response to David Kitt's 'Plato on Kinds of Animals.'" *Biology and Philosophy* 3 (1988): 592–96.

McPherran, Mark. *The Religion of Socrates*. University Park: Penn State University Press, 1999.

Menn, Stephen. "Aristotle and Plato on God as *Nous* and as the Good." *Review of Metaphysics* 45 (1992): 543–73.

Merki, Hubert. *Homoiosis Theoi*. Freiburg: Paulusverlag, 1952.

Mesquita, Antonio. "O Argumento Ontologico em Platao, I." *Philosophica* (1993): 31–42.

———. "O Argumento Ontologico em Platao, II." *Philosophica* (1994): 85–109.

Mikalson, Jon. *Athenian Popular Religion*. Chapel Hill: University of North Carolina Press, 1983.

Mohr, Richard. *The Platonic Cosmology*. Leiden: Brill, 1985.

———. "Plato's Theology Reconsidered: What the Demiurge Does." *History of Philosophy Quarterly* 2 (1985): 131–44.

Moltmann, Jurgen. *God in Creation*. San Francisco: Harper and Row, 1985.

More, P. E. *The Religion of Plato*. Princeton: Princeton University Press, 1921.

Moreau, Joseph. *L'Ame du monde de Platon aux Stoiciens*. Paris: Societe d'edition Les Belles Lettres, 1939.

Morgan, Kathryn. *Myth and Philosophy from the Pre-Socratics to Plato*. Cambridge: Cambridge University Press, 2000.

Morgan, Michael. *Platonic Piety*. New Haven: Yale University Press, 1990.

———. "Plato and Greek Religion." In Richard Kraut, ed., *The Cambridge Companion to Plato*. Cambridge: Cambridge University Press, 1992. Pp. 227–47.

Morrow, Glenn. "Necessity and Persuasion in Plato's *Timaeus*." *Philosophical Review* 59 (1950): 147–63.

Mueller, Gustav. "Plato and the Gods." *Philosophical Review* 45 (1936): 462–69.

Naddaf, Gerard. "Plato's *Theologia* Revisited." *Methexis* 9 (1996): 5–18.

Natorp, Paul. *Platos Ideenlehre*. Hamburg: Meiner, 1961.

Neal, Gordon, ed. *Plato's Sophist*. Manchester: Manchester University Press, 1975.

Neville, Robert. *God the Creator*. Chicago: University of Chicago Press, 1968.

———. *Soldier, Sage, Saint*. New York: Fordham University Press, 1978.

———. *Recovery of the Measure*. Albany: State University of New York Press, 1989.

———. *A Theology Primer*. Albany: State University of New York Press, 1991.

Nilsson, Martin. *A History of Greek Religion*. Oxford: Oxford University Press, 1952.

Nussbaum, Martha. *The Fragility of Goodness*. Cambridge: Cambridge University Press, 1986.

O'Connell, Robert. "God, Gods, and Moral Cosmos in Socrates' *Apology*." *International Philosophical Quarterly* 25 (1985): 31–50.

O'Leary-Hawthorne, Diane. "Not-Being and Linguistic Deception." *Apeiron* 29 (1996): 165–98.

O'Meara, Dominic. *Neoplatonism and Christian Thought*. Albany: State University of New York Press, 1982.

Origen. *On First Principles*. Gloucester, MA: Peter Smith, 1973.

Ostenfeld, Erik. "Self-Motion, Tripartition, and Embodiment." In Livio Rossetti, ed., *Understanding the "Phaedrus."* Sankt Augustin, Germany: Academia Verlag, 1992. Pp. 324–28.

———. "The Role and Status of the Forms in the *Timaeus*." In Thomas Calvo and Luc Brisson, eds., *Interpreting the "Timaeus-Critias."* Sankt Augustin, Germany: Academia Verlag, 1997. Pp. 167–77.

Owen, G. E. L. "Plato on Not-Being." In Gregory Vlastos, ed., *Plato*. Vol. 1. Garden City, NY: Anchor Books, 1970. Pp. 223–67.

Parry, Richard. "The Intelligible World-Animal in Plato's *Timaeus*." *Journal of the History of Philosophy* 29 (1991): 13–32.

Passmore, John. *The Perfectibility of Man*. London: Duckworth, 1970.

Patterson, Richard. "The Unique Worlds of the *Timaeus*." *Phoenix* 35 (1981): 105–19.

Pehrson, C. W. P. "Plato's Gods." *Polis* 9 (1990): 122–69.

Peikoff, Leonard. "Platonism's Inference from Logic to God." *International Studies in Philosophy* 16 (1984): 25–34.

Perl, Eric. "The Demiurge and the Forms: A Return to the Ancient Interpretation of Plato's Forms." *Ancient Philosophy* 18 (1998): 81–92.

Pittinger, Norman. *Catholic Faith in a Process Perspective*. Maryknoll, NY: Orbis Books, 1981.

Plato. *Laws*. Tr. A. E. Taylor. London: Dent, 1934.

———. *Platonis Opera*. Ed. John Burnet. 5 vols. Oxford: Clarendon, 1977.

———. *Plato's "Sophist."* Tr. Seth Bernadete. Chicago: University of Chicago Press, 1986.

———. *The Collected Dialogues of Plato*. Ed. Edith Hamilton and Huntington Cairns. Princeton: Princeton University Press, 1999.

Plutarch. *Plutarch's Morals*. Ed. William Goodwin. Boston: Little, Brown, 1870.

Press, Gerald, ed. *Who Speaks for Plato?* Lanham, MD: Rowman and Littlefield, 2000.

Prior, William. *Unity and Development in Plato's Metaphysics*. LaSalle, IL: Open Court, 1985.

Pritchard, Paul. "The Meaning of *Dynamis* at *Timaeus* 31C." *Phronesis* 35 (1990): 182–93.

Randall, John Herman. *Aristotle*. New York: Columbia University Press, 1960.

Reagan, James. "Being and Nonbeing in Plato's *Sophist*." *Modern Schoolman* 42 (1965): 305–14.

Reale, Giovanni. *Toward a New Interpretation of Plato*. Washington, DC: Catholic University of America Press, 1997.

Rexine, John. *Religion in Plato and Cicero*. New York: Philosophical Library, 1959.

Reydams-Schils, Gretchen. "Plato's World Soul." In Tomas Calvo and Luc Brisson, eds., *Interpreting the "Timaeus-Critias."* Sankt Augustin, Germany: Academia Verlag, 1997. Pp. 261–65.

Rist, John. "The Order of the Later Dialogues of Plato." *Phoenix* 14 (1960): 207–21.

Roberts, Jean. "The Problem about Being in the *Sophist*." *History of Philosophy Quarterly* 3 (1986): 229–43.

Robinson, J. M. *An Introduction to Early Greek Philosophy*. New York: Houghton Mifflin, 1968.

Robinson, T. M. "Understanding the *Timaeus*." *Proceedings of the Boston Area Colloquium in Ancient Philosophy* 2 (1986): 103–19.

———. "The Relative Dating of the *Timaeus* and *Phaedrus*." In Livio Rossetti, ed., *Understanding the "Phaedrus."* Sankt Augustin, Germany: Academia Verlag, 1992. Pp. 23–30.

Royce, Josiah. *The Philosophy of Loyalty*. New York: Macmillan, 1908.

Rue, Rachel. "The Philosopher in Flight: The Digression (172C–177C) in the *Theaetetus*." *Oxford Studies in Ancient Philosophy* 10 (1993): 71–100.

Russell, Bertrand. "Knowledge by Acquaintance and Knowledge by Description." In *The Basic Writings of Bertrand Russell*. New York: Simon and Schuster, 1961. Pp. 217–24.

Russell, Daniel. "Virtue as 'Likeness to God' in Plato and Seneca." *Journal of the History of Philosophy*. Forthcoming.

Rust, Alois. *Die Organismische Kosmologie von Alfred N. Whitehead*. Frankfurt: Athenaum, 1987.

Rutenber, Culbert. *The Doctrine of the Imitation of God in Plato*. New York: King's Crown, 1946.

Santayana, George. *Platonism and the Spiritual Life*. New York: Scribner's, 1927.

Sayre, Kenneth. "Plato's *Parmenides*: Why the Eight Hypotheses Are Not Contradictory." *Phronesis* 23 (1978): 133–50.

———. "Why Plato Never Had a Theory of Forms." *Proceedings of the Boston Area Colloquium in Ancient Philosophy* 9 (1993): 167–99.

———. *Plato's Literary Garden: How to Read a Platonic Dialogue*. Notre Dame: University of Notre Dame Press, 1995.

Schoenly, Steven. "The Etymologies of the Names of the Gods: *Cratylus* 400D–404B." *Dialogue* 16 (1974): 44–53.

Sedley, David. "'Becoming like God' in the *Timaeus* and Aristotle." In Thomas Calvo and Luc Brisson, eds. *Interpreting the "Timaeus-Critias."* Sankt Augustin, Germany: Academia Verlag, 1997. Pp. 327–39.

———. "The Ideal of Godlikeness." In Gail Fine, ed., *Plato*. Vol. 2. Oxford: Oxford University Press, 1999. Pp. 309–28.

Seeskin, Kenneth. "Platonism, Mysticism, and Madness." *Monist* 59 (1976): 574–86.

Sellars, Roy Wood. "Philosophy of Organism and Physical Realism." In P. A. Schilpp, ed., *The Philosophy of Alfred North Whitehead*. LaSalle, IL: Open Court, 1951. Pp. 407–33.

Sherburne, Donald. *A Key to Whitehead's "Process and Reality."* New York: Macmillan, 1966.

Shorey, Paul. *What Plato Said*. Chicago: University of Chicago Press, 1933.

Simon, Derek. "The *Sophist*, 246A–259E: *Ousia* and *to On* in Plato's Ontologies." *De Philosophia* 12 (1995–1996): 155–77.

Skemp, J. B. *The Theory of Motion in Plato's Later Dialogues*. Amsterdam: Hakkert, 1967.

Smith, Nicholas. "Platonic Scholars and Other Wishful Thinkers." In James Klagge and Nicholas Smith, eds., *Methods of Interpreting Plato and His Dialogues*. Oxford: Clarendon, 1992. Pp. 245–59.

Smith, Nicholas, and Paul Woodruff, eds. *Reason and Religion in Socratic Philosophy*. Oxford: Oxford University Press, 2000.

Solmsen, Friedrich. *Plato's Theology*. Ithaca: Cornell University Press, 1942.

———. "Greek Philosophy and the Discovery of Nerves." *Museum Helveticum* 18 (1961): 150–167, 169–97.

Sontag, Frederick. "The Faces of God." *Man and World* 8 (1975): 70–81.

Souilhe, Joseph. *Etude sur le terme "Dynamis" dans les dialogues de Platon*. Paris: Alcan, 1919.

Stace, W. T. *Mysticism and Philosophy*. London: Macmillan, 1960.

Stead, George. *Divine Substance*. Oxford: Clarendon, 1977.

Stenzel, Julius. *Plato's Method of Dialectic*. Oxford: Clarendon, 1940.

Taylor, A. E. "Whitehead's Philosophy of Religion." *The Dublin Review* 181 (July, 1927): 17–41.

———. *A Commentary on Plato's "Timaeus."* Oxford: Clarendon, 1928.

———. *Platonism and Its Influence*. New York: Longmans, Green, 1932.

———. *Plato: The Man and His Work*. New York: Dial, 1936.

———. "The "Polytheism" of Plato: An Apologia." *Mind* 47 (1938): 183–84.

Thesleff, Holger. "Platonic Chronology." *Phronesis* 34 (1989): 1–26.

Turnbull, Robert. *The "Parmenides" and Plato's Late Philosophy*. Toronto: University of Toronto Press, 1998.

Van Riel, Gerd. *Plato's Gods*. Burlington, VT: Ashgate, Forthcoming.

Viney, Donald. *Charles Hartshorne and the Existence of God*. Albany: State University of New York Press, 1985.

Vlastos, Gregory. *Plato's Universe*. Seattle: University of Washington Press, 1975.

Voegelin, Eric. *Order and History*. Vol. 3. Baton Rouge: Louisiana State University Press, 1957.

Voskuil, Duane. "Hartshorne, God, and Metaphysics: How the Cosmically Inclusive Personal Nexus and the World Interact." *Process Studies* 28 (1999): 212–28.

Watson, Gerard. "The Theology of Plato and Aristotle." *Irish Theological Quarterly* 37 (1970): 56–64.

Weiss, Paul. *Reality*. Princeton: Princeton University Press, 1938.

———. *Modes of Being*. Carbondale: Southern Illinois University Press, 1958.

———. *The God We Seek*. Carbondale: Southern Illinois University Press, 1964.

Whitehead, Alfred North. *The Aims of Education*. New York: Free Press, 1929.

———. *The Function of Reason*. Boston: Beacon, 1929.

———. *Modes of Thought*. New York: Macmillan, 1938.

———. "Mathematics and the Good." In P. A. Schilpp, ed., *The Philosophy of Alfred North Whitehead*. LaSalle, IL: Open Court, 1951. Pp. 666–81.

———. *Dialogues of Alfred North Whitehead*. Boston: Little, Brown, 1954.

———. *Science and the Modern World*. New York: Macmillan, 1957.

———. *Adventures of Ideas*. New York: Free Press, 1961.

———. *Process and Reality*. Corrected ed. New York: Free Press, 1978.

Whittemore, Robert. "Panentheism in Neo-Platonism." *Tulane Studies in Philosophy* 15 (1966): 47–70.

———. "The Proper Categorization of Plato's Demiurgos." *Tulane Studies in Philosophy* 27 (1978): 163–66.

Wiggins, David. "Sentence Meaning, Negation, and Plato's Problem of Non-Being." In Gregory Vlastos, ed., *Plato*. Vol. 1. Garden City, New York: Anchor Books, 1970. Pp. 268–303.

Wilamowitz-Moellendorff, Ulrich von. *Platon*. Vol. 1. Berlin: Weidmann, 1920.

Wild, John. "Plato and Christianity." *The Journal of Bible and Religion* 17 (1949): 3–16.

———. "Review of *The Doctrine of the Imitation of God in Plato*." *Journal of Religion* 29 (1949): 75.

Wolfson, Harry. *The Philosophy of Spinoza*. Cambridge: Harvard University Press, 1934.

———. "Extradeical and Intradeical Interpretations of Platonic Ideas." In *Religious Philosophy*. Cambridge: Harvard University Press, 1961.

Wordsworth, William. *Poetical Works*. Oxford: Oxford University Press, 1981.

Zeyl, Donald. "Commentary on 'Understanding the *Timaeus*.'" *Proceedings of the Boston Area Colloquium in Ancient Philosophy* 2 (1986): 120–25.

Index